Sant Jñāneśwara's

Pasāyadāna

Divine Blessings

Sant Jñāneśwara's
PASĀYADĀNA

(DIVINE BLESSINGS)

Original Commentary in Marathi
SHRI SHANKAR MAHARAJ KHANDARKAR

Editor
DR. SHRIKRISHNA DESHMUKH

Translator
MUKTA WALVEKAR

MOTILAL BANARSIDASS
SINCE 1903 IN INDOLOGY

First Edition : Delhi, 2018

ISBN : 978-81-208-4208-3

Also available at

MOTILAL BANARSIDASS
40-41 U.A. Bungalow Road, Jawahar Nagar, Delhi 110 007
1 B, J.S. Compound, Kennedy Bridge, Nana Chowk, Mumbai 400 007
203 Royapettah High Road, Mylapore, Chennai 600 004
236, 9th Main III Block, Jayanagar, Bengaluru 560 011
8 Camac Street, Kolkata 700 017
Ashok Rajpath, Patna 800 004
Chowk, Varanasi 221001

MLBD Cataloging-in-Publication Data

Sant Jñāneśwara's Pasāyadāna: *Divine Blessings*
by Sri Shankar Maharaj Khandarkar
ISBN : 978-81-208-4208-3
I. Saints and Teaching of India II. Sant Jñāneśwara
III. Pasāyadāna IV. Khandarkar, Shri Shankar Maharaj
V. Deshmukh, Shrikrishna VI. Walvekar, Mukta

Published by

Motilal Banarsidass Publishers Private Limited
www.mlbd.com • *mlbd@mlbd.com*
Printed by Replika Press Pvt. Ltd.

Sant Jñāneśwara

The Composer of Pasāyadāna

~ A Prayer for the Well-being of Humanity ~

(1275-1296, Alandi, Maharashtra)

Acknowledgement

Pasāyadāna, Sant Jñāneśwara's sublime prayer for the well-being of humanity, is one of the most valuable sources of learning available to us today. It provides timeless guidance for living a perfectly peaceful, blissful and meaningful life in the modern age. Translating this illumining commentary on Pasāyadāna has indeed been a profound, enriching and eye-opening experience for me.

Many people worked with great diligence and selflessness to create this book. My sincere thanks to *Dr. Jyotsna Patankar* and *Irina Derwall* for their tireless help in proofreading the translation, *Mrs. Sonali Phadke* for her dedicated efforts to create insightful cover design and *Mr. Pramod Walvekar* for his meticulous work in designing the book.

I am deeply indebted to my revered Sadguru **Dr. Shrikrishna Deshmukh** for his priceless guidance in every aspect of life. This translation is only a result of his constant inspiration, motivation and Supreme Grace!

Mrs. Mukta Walvekar

(Translator)

CONTENTS

PREFACE

जगाच्या कल्याणा संतांच्या विभूती ॥

Jagācyā kalyāṇā saṅtāṅcyā vibhūtī I

- 'Saints are born for the welfare of one and all.'

This is a famous quote by Sant Tukārāma, which explains the remarkable purpose of the life of saints. However, there is a misconception that saints are recluses and preachers from ivory towers, who disregard the society. They are blamed for promoting the path of renunciation and obstructing the overall materialistic progress of the nation. They are considered as mere eccentrics who go on pilgrimages, sing, chant, read, write and give spiritual discourses. Many people believe that India would have progressed much ahead of other nations if saints had used their intellect in the field of Science and Technology. By expounding the path of spirituality, devotion, righteousness, renunciation and detachment, saints have crippled the nation. However, this reproach is totally unfounded. The profound texts written by all saints testify the fact that they are deeply and genuinely concerned about the well-rounded progress of mankind.

Sant Jñāneśwara is a distinguished and luminary saint from Maharashtra. He is best known for his treatise Jñāneśwarī, which is a magnificent Marathi commentary on the Bhagvad-Gītā. At the end, Sant Jñāneśwara dedicated the treatise to his Guru Sant Nivṛttinātha and asked for Divine Blessings (Pasāyadāna), which is a topic of great warmth, affection and inclusiveness. However, he did not request anything for himself. Instead, he asked for Divine Blessings (Pasāyadāna) for the welfare of the entire Universe. Jñāneśwara Mahārāja had a sublime wish that the world should be pure, noble, pristine, auspicious and beautiful place. His eminent wish is expressed in Pasāyadāna. His prayer is for the prosperity of one and all. Such gracious, all-inclusive thoughts cannot be found in the literature of the so-called progressive culture of any other nation.

Human life cannot be evaluated just in terms of scientific, technological and commercial progress. The well-rounded and elevated human life is not dependent on the use of more or better tools and resources. The negative traits in human mind such as lust, anger, greed, arrogance, temptation, jealousy and vanity cannot be eradicated even with the most sophisticated scientific instruments. However, for maintaining the healthy state of the society, it is imperative that such mental disorders are completely wiped out.

Sciences and material objects can only enhance and beautify the external form of the world. They can fulfill the gross, physical needs of human existence. But they cannot guide humans to purity and the Ultimate Truth

(Satya, सत्य). External beauty, without purity and knowledge, is of no use to the real progress of the society. A young girl may look very beautiful with the help of cosmetic aids and advanced beauty treatments. But if she is bedridden with tuberculosis, none of the other finer things such as ornaments, cosmetics, food, clothes, etc. will help her. Similarly, if a society is afflicted with mental disorders such as lust, anger and greed, it suffers from the tuberculosis of unrighteousness. When a society frantically heads towards material progress, it is bound to find itself in a rat-race that leads to unethical, disgraceful, unreligious and utterly selfish behavior. This in turn causes tyranny, oppression, brutality and complete disregard for the sufferings of others. In such an unjust state, even if the society is bedecked with modern scientific tools and resources, it doesn't lead to stable, secure, virtuous and blissful living. Hence, the faith in Religion and God is imperative in the society.

Science, Religion, and God are inherently different entities, but they are complementary to each other. When woven together, they make human life truthful, auspicious and beautiful (Satya, Śiva, Sundara; सत्य, शिव, सुंदर).

1. **Science** makes the world beautiful (Sundara, सुंदर) and comfortable place to live in. However, Science is neither auspicious nor the Eternal Truth. Science is beneficial in the form of

instruments, and killer in the form of weapons. It is a boon in the form of creation as well as a curse in the form of destruction. It cannot lead the world towards the ultimate welfare of mankind. Science is always evolving, hence incomplete in nature. It is changeable and will ultimately come to an end with the Universe.

2. **Religion** is auspicious (Śiva, शिव). Following the guidelines of Religion leads to more tolerance, affinity, compassion, harmony and security. But it is neither beautiful nor the Eternal truth. The practice of Religion is arduous and painful. Hence, there is no beauty in it. Following Religion involves actions, which can only be executed by the body, organs or the mind, which are perishable. Hence, Religion cannot be the changeless, Eternal Truth (Satya, सत्य).
3. **God** is the only changeless and Eternal Truth (Satya, सत्य), which is not dependent on any other person or object. The quest for the God makes human life more purposeful, meaningful, steadfast, and fruitful. He is the substratum (Adhiṣṭhāna, अधिष्ठान) of both Science and Religion. God is the original proponent of Science, since fundamentals of Science are seen in the process of creation of the world. God is the institutor of Religion. In fact, the very goal of Religion is the realization of the God.

Religion, in today's world, mainly indicates Duty-Based Religion (Swadharma, स्वधर्म). It is an intermediary between Science and the God. If people in the field of Science and Technology are faithful to their own duties (religious), then they work sincerely and conscientiously. They boost the production and productivity without being deceitful. A weapon is best used when it is given to brave soldiers instead of naive young children. Similarly, Science can be best used only by the dutiful and compliant scientists, researchers and technologists. If all professional people such as pilots, teachers, drivers, doctors, lawyers, engineers, owners and workers are faithful, meticulous, compassionate, sincere and trustworthy, then Technology in their respective fields can be immensely beneficial to the mankind. Sincere execution of self-duties (following Religion) purifies the mind and helps in comprehending the real nature of the God. Thus, Religion is an intermediary between Science and the God.

Life in the 21st century is very busy, complex and fast-paced. Society is being transformed very swiftly, like never before. People are crossing boundaries established by the old concepts of Religion and righteousness and entering the new realm of Science based on intelligentsia. But this new-age, modern thinking is not completely accurate. Even amid the fast-paced life, we need to understand the importance of staying anchored to a firm, secure ground.

For example, the body may be roaming or working, but the embodied soul (Jīva, जीव), stays stable in its residence (body). The stable embodied-soul is the very reason why body continues to move and function. When the embodied soul leaves the body, the body becomes insentient and dies consequently.

Similarly, righteous and dutiful (religious) life is the foundation of a healthy, strong society. It is perfectly fine if new scientific inventions and economic development bring rapid action, progress and evolution in the society. But the fundamental values of dutifulness and righteousness must be cultivated in any era to keep the society firmly rooted in the ground.

In the absence of code of moral conduct and righteousness, nations start competing and fighting against each other. Owners and workers get into financial brawls. Rulers and ordinary citizens live in a perturbed state. There is a lack of friendliness, empathy and compassion for each other. Fear, frustration, violence, torment, discontent and afflicting laws proliferate and rule the society. Even honest people find it impossible to enjoy their hard-earned wealth. Friction can be seen at all levels in the society. Master-servant, teacher-student, landlord-tenant, father-son, leader-follower, Hindu-Muslim are some of the joints of friction. Even the most educated and advanced societies have such joints, and they creak more with acceleration. Any greasing by extrinsic laws, rules and regulations only intensifies the creaking and eventually breaks the system. This hampers the very speed and pace of life, of which human beings are so proud these days. In such a society, life is eventually reduced to the state of chaos, indignity, turmoil and ultimately destruction.

The external form of the world may rapidly transform with the help of Science. Saints have no objection to materialistic progress and evolution. Travelling by an airplane is surely more efficient than walking the same long distance. Staying in a spacious palace instead of a poor hut is certainly a finer aspect of life. Growth in this extrinsic direction is a great transformation. But it should not be at the expense of fundamental human values and the quest for the Ultimate Truth (Satya, सत्य). When the path of righteousness is not followed, people indulge in activities such as infidelity, stealing, bribing, corruption and violence. Such rapid, unrestrained progress is bound to spell the destruction of the society, which is evidently happening today.

Thus, so far it is clear that Science, Religion and Self-realization (the quest for the Ultimate Truth) - all three together are necessary for human development in a real sense. One is incomplete without the other. A woman may be both beautiful and pure, but if she is ignorant about the real nature of her Self, she will not attain the ultimate goal of human life, i.e. Self-realization. Sītā, the wife of Lord Rāma is an example of an ideal woman. She was the perfect combination of exquisite beauty, purity, loyal dedication to Rāma and the knowledge that Lord Rāma is the Eternal truth, i.e. Brahman.

Sant Jñāneśwara had a sublime wish that these qualities of Sītā proliferate everywhere in the entire world. His wishes are expressed in the following verses of Pasāyadāna -

1. **जो जे वांछील तो तें लाहो । प्राणिजात ॥** (3)
   Jo je vāñchīla to teṁ lāho / Prāṇijāta //
   - 'May everyone get what he or she wishes for.'

Science and material resources beautify the world. Everyone should be able to fulfill his desires and attain the worldly prosperity. The verse indicates this noble, all-inclusive wish by Sant Jñāneśwara.

2. **जें खळांची व्यंकटी सांडो । तया सत्कर्मी- रती वाढो ॥** (2)
   Jeṁ khaḻāñcī vyaṅkaṭī sāṅḍo / Tayā satkarmī ratī vāḍho/
   - 'May the evil people lose their viciousness; may they gradually get interested in noble deeds.'

   दुरितांचे तिमिर जावो । विश्व स्वधर्मसूर्यें पाहो । (3)
   Duritāñce timira jāvo / Viśva svadharmasūryeṁ pāho /
   - 'May the sun of following one's duties (Swadharma, स्वधर्म) enlighten this world.'

   वर्षत सकळमंगळी । ईश्वरनिष्ठांची मांदियाळी ।
   अनवरत भूमंडळी । भेटो तया भूतां ॥ (4)

Varṣata sakaḻa maṅgaḻī | Īśvaraniśṭhāñcī māṅdiyāḻī |
Anavarata bhūmaṅḍaḻī | Bheṭo tayā bhūtāṁ|
- 'May all saints be our kith and kin, may all people praise and worship God throughout their life, may all people follow the teachings of the saints, so that all will realize God.'

Soiled clothes need to be first cleaned, only then they can be colored as desired. Similarly, dirt, impurity, negativities and viciousness in the mind need to be first cleaned up. Meticulous execution of one's own duties (Swadharma, स्वधर्म) is the best way to cleanse the mind. Saints create guidelines for following duties that are in sync with the era and times. Following teachings of saints will make the world pure, clean, glorious and pristine place for living. This wish is reflected in the verses mentioned above. Jñāneśwara Mahārāja wishes to bring this ultimate noble reality within the reach of mankind.

3. ते सर्वांही सदा सज्जन । सोयरे होतु ॥ (6)
Te sarvāṅhī sadā sajjana | Soyare hotu ||
- 'May the saints and their teachings be accepted, revered and loved by the society.'

भजिजो आदिपुरुखी । अखंडित ॥ (7)
Bhajijo ādipurukhī | Akhaṇḍita ||
- 'May we worship the Universal God.'

आणि ग्रंथोपजीविये । विशेषीं लोकीं इयें ।
दृष्टादृष्ट विजयें । होआवे जी ॥ (8)

Āṇi granṭhopajīviye / Viśeṣīṁ lokīṁ iyeṁ /
Dṛṣṭādṛṣṭa vijayeṁ / Hoāve jī //
- 'May the followers of divine and pious texts be victorious in this world and beyond.'

Human life should not be spent in just appreciating the external beauty in the world, nor should it be limited to just following the guidelines of righteousness or Swadharma. The ultimate welfare of mankind lies in realization of Brahman (Pure Bliss), which is perpetual, transcendental and absolute in nature. Enlightened saints realize Brahman as their real Self. Hence, it is necessary to consider saints as our close acquaintances, follow their teachings, pursue the quest for the Ultimate Truth, i.e. God (Brahman) and realize that Brahman is the true nature of the Self.

Jñāneśwara Mahārāja has evidently asked for these Divine Blessings (Pasāyadāna) to make the entire world a more beautiful, auspicious and truthful place. The society needs to possess these traits in every era. Thus, it is incorrect to say that saints are recluses or isolationists from the society. They may not have done new cutting-edge scientific innovations, but they neither opposed nor obstructed the evolution brought in by Science. Mankind surely needs new technological research and inventions. However, such discoveries are only gross, physical experiments w.r.t. intrinsic health and permanent welfare of the society. Any bright, intelligent person can conduct the physical experiments. Saints chose not to invest their subtle, astute, pure minds into materialistic progress, nor did they emphasize too much on it. They dwelled upon the internal, fundamental health of the society and cared deeply for making mankind stable, prosperous and happy intrinsically. They not only wrote scholarly texts about their vision, but also lived their own lives in accordance with the vision. Saints have consistently propounded dutiful life based on sincerity, righteousness, devotion and truthfulness.

The praising hymn (Āratī, आरती) written for Sant Jñāneśwara states that -

हित नेणती कोणी । अवतार पांडुरंग । नाव ठेवले ज्ञानी ॥

Hita neṇatī konī | Avatār Pāṇḍuranga | Nāva thevale Jñānī ||

The verse is truly appropriate in every sense of the word. It states that most ordinary people lead lives without really knowing where their best interests lie. Sant Jñāneśwara does the remarkable job of making people aware of their own welfare, hence he is named as Jñānī or Jñāneśwara (King of Knowledge).

Divine Blessings, the concluding part of the 18th chapter of Jñāneśwarī, has 9 poetic verses. Sant Jñāneśwara has prayed for 10 blessings through them. It contains the very gist of Jñāneśwarī. It includes axioms that reflect teachings from many branches of social science such as economics, politics, psychology,

Religion, devotion and the doctrine of Self-realization. Sant Jñāneśwara describes these teachings using beautiful, impressive and remarkable language in a slightly enigmatic manner. Pasāyadāna is highly beneficial even in today's age of democracy, both inside and outside of India. One can experience distinct, unusual happiness as he starts treading the path outlined by these verses, which in turn, expedites the progress on that path. If studied properly, Pasāyadāna can help the well-rounded evolution of a person on individual, familial and social fronts.

This commentary reflects my sincere, deep yearning for the welfare and prosperity of mankind. I share the earnest longing of Jñāneśwara Mahārāja for the well-being of everyone in this world. This commentary is based on the principles of Advaita Vedānta as propounded by Vedas and Upaniṣads. Various verses cited in the text underscore this fact. I pray to God to fulfill my earnest wish – '*May all people rectify and purify their perceptions, conduct, behavior and life-style after reading this commentary on Pasāyadāna.*'

Shri Shankar Maharaj Khandarkar
Pandharpur, Maharashtra

COMPOSITION

आता विश्वात्मकें देवें । येणे वाग्यज्ञें तोषावें ।
तोषोनिं मज द्यावे । पसायदान हें ॥ १ ॥

Ātā viśvātmakeṁ deveṁ | Yeṇe vāgyajñeṁ toṣāveṁ |
Toṣoniṁ maja dyāve | Pasāyadāna heṁ || 1 ||

- 'Now, may the Lord of the Universe be pleased with this pious verbal worship. May He confer His Divine Blessings (Pasāyadāna, पसायदान) on me.'

जें खळांची व्यंकटी सांडो । तया सत्कर्मी- रती वाढो ।
भूतां परस्परे पडो । मैत्र जीवाचें ॥ २ ॥

Jeṁ khaḻāñcī vyaṅkaṭī sāṅḍo | Tayā satkarmī ratī vāḍho |
Bhūtāṁ paraspare paḍo | Maitra jīvācheṁ || 2 ||

- 'May vicious people get rid of their evilness and be gradually inclined to noble deeds. May all living beings be bonded with the ties of friendship.'

दुरितांचे तिमिर जावो । विश्व स्वधर्मसूर्यें पाहो ।
जो जे वांछील तो तें लाहो । प्राणिजात ॥ ३ ॥

Duritāñce timira jāvo | Viśva svadharmasūryeṁ pāho |
Jo je vāñchīla to teṁ lāho | Prāṇijāta || 3 ||

- 'May the darkness of sins go away. May the sun of Swadharma (स्वधर्म, Duty-Based Religion) rise on the Universe. May everyone attain what he aspires for.'

वर्षत सकळमंगळी । ईश्वरनिष्ठांची मांदियाळी ।
अनवरत भूमंडळी । भेटो तया भूतां ॥ ४ ॥

Varṣata saka̱la maṅga̱lī / Īśvaraniṣṭhāñcī māṅdiyā̱lī /
Anavarata bhūmaṅḍa̱lī / Bheṭo tayā bhūtāṁ // 4 //

- 'May everyone meet the enlightened saints, who shower their brilliant teachings all over the Universe.'

चलां कल्पतरूंचे आरव । चेतना चिंतामणींचें गाव ।
बोलते जे अर्णव । पीयूषाचे ॥ ५ ॥
चंद्रमें जे अलांछन । मार्तंड जे तापहीन ।
ते सर्वांही सदा सज्जन । सोयरे होतु ॥ ६ ॥

Calāṁ kalpatarūṅce ārava /
Cetanā ciṅtāmaṇīṅcem̐ gāva /
Bolate je arṇava / Pīyūṣhāce // 5 //
Caṅdrame je alāṅchana / Mārtaṅḍa je tāpahīna /
Te sarvāṅhī sadā sajjana / Soyare hotu // 6 //

- 'The grandeur, brilliance and timelessness of saints transcends that of Kalpataru, Cintāmaṇi, ocean, moon and sun. Hence saints and their teachings should be accepted, revered and loved by the society.'

किंबहुना सर्व सुखी । पूर्ण होऊनि तिहीं लोकी ।
भजिजो आदिपुरुखी । अखंडित ॥ ७ ॥

Kiṁbahunā sarva sukhī / Pūrṇa hoūni tinhīṁ lokī /
Bhajijo ādipurukhī / Akhaṇḍita // 7 //

- 'People from all three worlds should worship the Universal God for achieving happiness on all fronts.'

आणि ग्रंथोपजीविये । विशेषीं लोकीं इयें ।
दृष्टादृष्ट विजयें । होआवे जी ॥ ८ ॥

Āṇi granṭhopajīviye | Viśeṣīṁ lokīṁ iyeṁ |
Dṛṣṭādṛṣṭa vijayeṁ | Hoāve jī || 8 ||

- 'Followers of divine and pious texts should be victorious in this world and beyond.'

येथ म्हणे श्रीविश्वेशरावो । हा होईल दानपसावो ।
येणें वरें ज्ञानदेवो । सुखिया जाला ॥ ९ ॥

Yetha mhaṇe śrī Viśveśarāvo | Hā hoīla dāna pasāvo |
Yeṇeṁ vareṁ Jṅyānadevo | Sukhiyā jālā || 9 ||

- 'Here Sant Nivṛttinātha said to Sant Jñāneśwara that his prayers will indeed be heard and fulfilled. With this divine, blissful grace from Sadguru, Sant Jñāneśwara became truly gratified and happy.'

BACKGROUND

आता विश्वात्मकें देवें । येणे वाग्यज्ञें तोषावें ।
तोषोनिं मज द्यावे । पसायदान हें ॥ १ ॥

Ātā viśvātmakeṁ deveṁ / Yeṇe vāgyajṅeṁ toṣāveṁ /
Toṣoniṁ maja dyāve / Pasāyadāna heṁ // 1 //

- 'Now, may the Universal Lord be pleased with this pious verbal worship. May He confer his Divine Blessings (Pasāyadāna, पसायदान) on me.'

Jñāneśwara Mahārāja wrote a magnificent treatise on Bhagvad-Gītā in Marathi to please his Guru Sant Nivṛttinātha, and to show the path of the supreme welfare to mankind. Eminent saints like Nāmdeva and Eknātha praised this treatise with titles such as 'the illumining commentary' (Bhāvārtha Dīpikā, भावार्थ दीपिका), 'an ornament of Gītā' (Gītālaṅkāra, गीतालंकार), 'the ripples of Pure Bliss' (Brahmānandalaharī, ब्रह्मानंदलहरी), 'the light showing the realm of Self-realization' (Brahma Samrājya Dīpikā, ब्रह्मसाम्राज्यदीपिका) etc. Sant Jñāneśwara has himself named it lovingly as 'the chanting of Religion' (DharmaSaṅkīrtana, धर्मसंकीर्तन). He has also honored his Guru Nivṛttinātha with great adjectives such as 'the blooming of the lotus of knowledge' (Vidyāraviṅdaprabodha, विद्यारविंदप्रबोध) and 'expert exponent' (Viśadabodhavidagdha, विशदबोधविदग्ध).

Sant Jñāneśwara is evidently a gifted and prolific poet. While asking for Divine Blessings, he refers to his Guru as 'the Lord who is the soul of the Universe' (Viśvātmaka Deva, विश्वात्मक देव), and his own commentary on Bhagvad-Gītā as 'the verbal worship' (वाग्यज्ञ, Vāgyajña). These words are indeed profound and insightful.

Lord Kṛṣṇa has said in Bhagvad-Gītā -

इष्टान्भोगान्हि वो देवा दास्यन्ते यज्ञभाविताः ।

Iṣṭān bhogānhi vo devā dāsyante yajña-bhāvitāḥ |

- 'The Gods pleased with worship (yajña, यज्ञ) will bestow all the desired comforts.'

Sant Jñāneśwara evidently follows the same thought at the end of his commentary to ask for Divine Blessings from his Guru.

Nivṛttinātha was an incarnation of Lord Mahādeva, i.e. Śaṅkara. Rudrasūtktas have referred to Lord Śaṅkara as the Universal Form (Viśvarūpa, विश्वरूप). Thus, Nivṛttinātha was the vast, expansive Universal Lord, who would be certainly pleased with the verbal worship of Jñāneśwarī. Keeping this in mind, Sant Jñāneśwara expresses his wish in the first verse of Pasāyadāna-

आता विश्वात्मकें देवें ।

Ātā viśvātmakeṁ deveṁ |

- 'Now, Oh Lord in the Universal Form!'

The word 'Now' indicates that Jñāneśwarī is now completed. Sant Jñāneśwara says, 'Let the Universal

Lord in the form of Nivṛttinātha be pleased with this commentary on Bhagvad-Gītā and bestow the Divine Blessings upon me.'

Here, Saint Nivṛttinātha has been addressed as 'the Lord in the Universal Form' (Viśvātmak Deva, विश्वात्मक देव), which has five possible meanings -

1. Pervades the Universe in the form of Brahman
2. Accepts (the responsibility of) the Universe through its creation, maintenance and destruction
3. Enjoys the Universe through five senses
4. Permeates the Universe completely by being the very source of its existence and illumination.
5. One whose soul is the Universe

There is a verse from Upaniṣad, which says -

यत्र त्वस्य सर्वमात्मैवाभूत् ।

Yatra tvasya Sarvamātmaivābhūt / (Bṛi. Up. 4.5.15)

- '(An enlightened person is the) One whose very soul is this vast, expansive Universe.'

Nivṛttinātha was a Self-realized saint, whose very soul was this Universe. All the five meanings mentioned above befit him perfectly. There is a complete unanimity between Him and the Universal Lord. This is precisely why he was able to bestow the Divine Blessings. Any person, who considers himself limited to the form of his body, cannot have the power, knowledge or authority to grant such a noble, all-encompassing blessing. The extraordinary ability to confer these supreme blessings has been beautifully conveyed with the help of the words 'the Lord in the Universal Form' by Sant Jñāneśwara.

येणे वाग्यज्ञें तोषावें ।

Yeṇe vāgyajñeṁ toṣāveṁ |

- 'May Him (Nivṛttināatha, the Lord in the Universal Form) be pleased with the offering of this verbal yajña (यज्ञ, worship), i.e. Jñāneśwarī.'

The word 'yajña' in this verse suggests three meanings -

1. **Keeping consistency** -

   Sant Jñāneśwara has written his commentary by being consistent with the core theme of original Bhagvad-Gītā. The teachings of his Guru Sant Nivṛttināatha were reproduced accurately in the form of this treatise.

2. **Offerings** -

   With utmost faith, Sant Jñāneśwara offers flowers (verses in his commentary) at the feet of the Universal Lord. The verses of Jñāneśwarī are deeply meaningful and insightful. They are exquisitely brilliant and teach unfaltering philosophy. These offerings to Guru are a form of yajña.

3. **Worship** -

   Sant Jñāneśwara says, 'And now I surrender myself at the feet of my Guru Nivṛttināatha and worship him with my verbal yajña.'

Jñāneśwara Mahārāja has referred to his treatise as 'the worship by words'. Any learned person, who writes this type of magnificent work should follow this example and regard his work as worship to the Lord, so that readers do not go astray from the path of faith.

Sant Jñāneśwara, who calls himself as the son and the servant of Sant Nivṛttinātha, has extensively praised his Guru with complete surrender and sincere devotion at the beginning of almost all chapters in Jñāneśwarī. That is precisely why he was eligible to ask for the Divine Blessings from his Guru.

तोषोनिं मज द्यावे । पसायदान हें ॥

Toṣoniṁ maja dyāve | Pasāyadāna heṁ ||

- 'Satisfied as He is, He may bestow upon me the Divine Blessings.'

Sant Jñāneśwara has surely asked for something in return of his verbal worship. But it is not for his personal health, wealth, success or family. His prayer is for the welfare and prosperity of the world, which illustrates his nobility, grandeur, benevolence, saintly eminence and all-embracing generous attitude.

PASĀYADĀNA IN A NEW LIGHT

Sant Jñāneśwara prayed for Divine Blessings from his Guru for the welfare of the entire Universe. His Guru agreed and granted him the blessings. However, is it limited to only the 'give and take' ritual between a Sadguru and his disciple? If it was pertinent to the interaction only between two of them, we would have seen a completely different picture of the Society in last 750 years. Vicious people would have eradicated their evilness and inclined to noble deeds just because of blessing by an enlightened Guru. All living beings would have bonded with each other with the ties of friendship. However, the state of the society seems completely opposite to this ideology. So, it has become necessary to look at Pasāyadāna in a new light.

There is a saying – 'Nobody reaches where he has reached until he has what it takes.' A person can reach the intended goal only when he has all necessary qualities and requisites to achieve the goal. Sant Jñāneśwara has clearly outlined the (spiritual) goal in his commentary on Bhagvad-Gītā. He says -

येथ अविद्यानाशु हें स्थळ । तेणें मोक्षोपादान फळ ।
या दोहीं केवळ । साधन ज्ञान ॥

Yetha avidyānashu heṃ sthala/Teneṃ mokśopadāna phala / Yā dohiṃ keval / Sādhana jñāna // (18.1243)

- '**Sat-Cit-Ānanda** (सत्-चित्-आनंद) Brahman is the nature of all beings. However, we still identify ourselves with body and its attributes (such as height, color, gender etc.). This is called as ignorance or bondage (Avidyā, अविद्या). To eradicate Avidyā and achieve liberation (Mokṣa, मोक्ष) we must realize the Pure Knowledge of Ātman. This is the ultimate goal of human life.'

Sant Jñāneśwara has expounded this one topic in many ways in his treatise.

A seeker who studies Jñāneśwarī should honestly follow the same intent with which it was originally written. He should focus on what Sant Jñāneśwara intends to give through his treatise, rather than what the seeker himself is trying to search for. Pasāyadāna outlines the list of requisites needed to achieve the goal of Mokṣa. The central message in Jñāneśwarī is presented in the form of aphorisms (Sūtra, सूत्र) in 9 verses of Pasāyadāna. **These verses are meant to make the seeker cognizant of his own responsibilities in the path of liberation.**

Blessings are generally asked from higher power like Īśvara or Guru. However, the treatise of Jñāneśwarī was written for welfare of all people. It seems only logical that these prayers indicate the commitment asked from people (readers) for their own upliftment. Readers should first strive to change their behavior intrinsically as per the guidance in this text. Sant Jñāneśwara has referred to all seekers as incarnations of the God (Maheśa-Mūrti, महेश-मूर्ति), so he would not order people to do anything authoritatively. But in the process of asking blessings from his Guru, he has essentially given a lot of responsibility to seekers (readers) and some responsibility to Īśvara (ईश्वर, God). Seekers should eradicate their own evil tendencies and Īśvara should make many groups of enlightened Saints available to the mankind.

Mere recitation, reading or singing of verses in Pasāyadāna has evidently not changed people or society. It is incorrect to passively rely on the divine power of Sant Jñāneśwara or Sant Nivṛttinātha and expect a magical change to take place in the mankind. The Indian mindset has resigned to constant expectations of blessings, grace or divine power in life. As a result, people have become dependent, lethargic, passive and actionless, which surely is an area of concern. It is only natural and right to expect people to evaluate their own malicious thoughts and eradicate their bad inclinations themselves. The darkness created by a person's sins can go away only by the light of his own virtues. The world will see the glorious light of actions (Swadharma) only when everyone performs his own duties in the most effective manner. It is clearly the responsibility of the reader to understand the meaning of these verses, introspect himself and change his own behavior intrinsically. If everyone can change himself in this manner, it may be called as the real fulfillment of Sant Jñāneśwara's wishes in Pasāyadāna.

Being righteous, religious, virtuous, cordial and friendly are good qualities that are necessary in life. One is expected to attain these qualities after careful study of Pasāyadāna. They are prerequisites to attain liberation. However, we must know that they are all preparative actions, not end goal in themselves. One should not limit himself to acquiring these qualities. It is important to ultimately evolve to the stage of Self-realization (Mokṣa or liberation). If a genuine, upright seeker is not conscious, his ego may inflate with thoughts such as 'I am righteous', 'I am virtuous', etc. Even the society praises such a well-behaved person. These fascinating attractions entice the seeker and keep him stranded in his bindings. So long as a person feels 'I am something', he cannot realize his real Self as Brahman. In the last phase of spiritual pursuit, even the thought that 'I am Brahman' is considered obstructive. Thus, the reader of Pasāyadāna has an additional responsibility to not get carried away in these preliminary qualifications and consciously pursue the goal of Self-realization.

FIRST PRAYER

The second verse in Pasāyadāna has three prayers. The verse is -

जें खळांची व्यंकटी सांडो । तया सत्कर्मी- रती वाढो ।
भूतां परस्परे पडो । मैत्र जीवाचें ॥ २ ॥

Jeṁ khaḻāñcī vyaṅkaṭī sāṅḍo | Tayā satkarmī ratī vāḍho |
Bhūtāṁ paraspare paḍo | Maitra jīvācheṁ || 2 ||

- 'May vicious people get rid of their evilness and be gradually inclined to noble deeds. May all living beings be bonded with the ties of friendship.'

Sant Jñāneśwara has expressed a splendid wish in the 3rd verse of Pasāyadāna for the fulfillment of all desires of everyone in the world. However, the world is full of both good and bad people. One may think, it is disastrous if bad people are indeed bestowed with such fortunate blessings. Some sadistic people take pleasure in harassing the amiable, gentle people. A thief is hungry for the money that belongs to others, while a lustful person craves for someone other than his own spouse. Such immoral pursuits only spell ruin and humiliation. To address this issue, Sant Jñāneśwara has first prayed for complete elimination of evilness from the minds of vicious people.

जें खळांची व्यंकटी सांडो । (1st prayer)

Jeṁ khaḻāñcī vyaṅkaṭī sāṅḍo |

- 'May vicious people get rid of their evilness.'

Vicious people find happiness in evil and malicious actions. However, they don't realize that such actions ultimately lead to total disaster. They eclipse the saintly teachings with their sadistic mindset. They criticize, slander and enjoy hearing defamation of other people. They harass people, block their progress, speak harshly, amass illegal wealth, enforce others to follow the wrong path and vehemently try to destroy goodness from society. Their vicious actions make them detestable for one and all. The presence of even one evil person plagues his family, society and the nation at large.

Hence, Sant Jñāneśwara expresses his very first cordial wish – 'May vicious people lose their malicious nature, anger, greed, hatred, lust and other such dreadful traits.' Mankind cannot be purified in a true sense until viciousness is completely eradicated. Fulfillment of this blessing forms the very foundation of the progress of mankind.

Evil, sinister, wicked, immoral and blackguard are all synonyms of each other. The spectrum of evilness is huge.

- Some people feel implicitly tickled when others are in difficult situations.

- Some people are unjust or unfair to others for their own petty, selfish gains.
- Some people become happy when others suffer, and some people suffer when others are happy.
- Some people are ready to degrade others for their own pleasure. They may even go to any extent to cause pain to others.
- Some people become happy even when some stranger or a completely unrelated, third person is in pain.
- Some people feel delighted when their opponents or enemies are facing miseries in life.
- Some people behave in shrewd, cunning or deceiving manner to con others.
- Some people succumb to criminal, vindictive behavior and denounce the judicial system for their own greedy, atrocious satisfaction.

These malicious tendencies have proliferated in the society today and they clearly contradict the sublime wish expressed in this verse. It may not be possible to eradicate the complete spectrum of evilness from mankind. Mere singing of Pasāyadāna verses will not eradicate the wickedness. However, each one of us who reads this text, can surely analyze and evaluate our own behavior to discern the shades of wickedness present in our own mind.

For example, If I deceive a co-worker at work for my own promotion, it is evilness. If I unnecessarily hurt others with harsh words or rude behavior, it is evilness.

If I manipulate poor, illiterate people, it is evilness. If I find secret pleasure in seeing debacle of my acquaintances, it is evilness. If I accept bribe in any form to finish my assigned work, it is evilness. If I lie, cheat, delude or mislead others for my selfish gains, it is evilness.

In short, all of us have varying shades of wickedness inside us. We can introspect and strive to eradicate these traces of evilness. Sant Jñāneśwara wrote his glorious commentary only for upliftment of people. We must remember that he did not wish or ask anything for himself. He only wished to see the better state of society and it is the duty of the society today to grant these blessings to him. Even if we (readers) follow his teachings scrupulously, it will be a great step towards fulfillment of the sincere wish expressed by him.

The treatise of Bhagvad-Gītā or Jñāneśwarī can greatly assist to change the intrinsic mindset of people of all kinds. They provide clear guidelines on how to remove maliciousness from mind.

Lord Kṛṣṇa says -

ईश्वरः सर्वभूतानां हृद्देशेर्जुन तिष्ठति ॥

Īśvaraḥ sarvabhūtānām hṛddeśerjuna tiṣṭhati // (18.61)

- 'The Supreme Lord (Īśvara) resides within the hearts of all living beings.'

Similarly, Sant Jñāneśwara has defined the path of devotion (Bhakti, भक्ति) in a very expansive, all-inclusive manner by saying that 'one should find God in every being'.

This is the very gist of the theory of Advaita Vedānta. If every person is God or Kṛṣṇa or Brahman, then deceiving or hurting others essentially means deceiving or hurting ourselves. This is an intriguing thought. We can surely repress our own evil tendencies and benefit from this teaching. The wish expressed by Sant Jñāneśwara also includes removal of evilness from people who may not ever read his treatise.

SECOND PRAYER

As people turn away from evilness, they should be gradually inclined to noble and virtuous deeds. They must not return to evil actions. Sant Jñāneśwara, therefore, prays for the second blessing.

तया सत्कर्मी- रती वाढो । (2nd prayer)

Tayā satkarmī ratī vāḍho |

- 'May they be gradually inclined to noble deeds.'

As readers of Jñāneśwarī, it is our prime duty to not just feel content with 'not doing bad actions'. We should strive to perform progressively better, sublime work in life. Mere recitation of the verse in Pasāyadāna will not lead the entire society towards noble deeds. Each one of us has the onus to perform useful, productive, effective, virtuous and benevolent actions at our own level.

The word Satkarma (सत्कर्म) has a very vast, extensive meaning. The word 'Sat' generally stands for 'good'. Satkarma means 'good work'. However, 'Sat' ultimately means Brahman. Satkarma means executing all necessary actions for Self-realization or liberation. There should be no short-cuts, reluctance, latitude or inconsistency while working. We should strive to perform noble, righteous actions, but not stay limited to just doing basic good-work. For Self-realization, the actions need to be much more articulate, evolved, pure, profound and meaningful. According to Vedānta, when actions are done without the illusive attitude of doership (Kartṛtva Bhrānti, कर्तृत्व भ्रांति) in a selfless manner, they lead to complete purification of mind (Cittaśuddhi, चित्तशुद्धि). Only such pure and calm mind is eligible for the ultimate stage of Self-realization. Thus, the word Satkarma essentially denotes all actions required for purification of mind and Self-realization. It is our prime responsibility to understand the Law of Karma and act accordingly. However, not every action can be performed in a selfless manner. For better understanding, we may divide the types of actions into five categories.

Actions pertaining to body (Deha-Karma, देहकर्म)

It is the foremost duty of a person to keep his body clean and healthy. Maintaining optimistic outlook, enthusiastic approach, cheerfulness, readiness for hard-work, consistency and regular studies are all part of good health. There is a Sanskrit proverb that says,

शरीरमाद्यं खलु धर्मसाधनम् ।

Sharirmādyam khalu dharmasādhanam | –

- 'The body is the foremost important instrument for executing actions.'

Sant Samartha Rāmdāsa Swāmī has written an entire chapter in Dāsabodha named **Naradehastavana** (नरदेहस्तवन), which outlines the immense value of being born as a human being. Gross body is coupled with the mind, so it is important to nurture good, virtuous thoughts and desires in the mind as well. A healthy body and positive mind are needed to perform all other actions required for spiritual pursuit. Practices such as chanting of a Mantra and meditation require that the seeker is able to sit in one given posture (Āsana, आसन) for a long duration. It is imperative to have a fit body and stable mind for that purpose. A seeker should strive to acquire divine qualities and eradicate demoniac traits as outlined in the 16th chapter of Bhagvad-Gītā. Samartha Rāmdāsa Swāmī has described the concept of 'an ideal person' (Uttam Puruṣa, उत्तम पुरूष) in Dāsabodha. Every seeker should strive to become ideal person by making the best possible use of his human body and human life. It is important to consider actions pertaining to one's own body as part of Satkarma, since they eventually help in Self-realization.

Job / business (Vyavasāya-Karma, व्यवसायकर्म)

Work is an integral part of human life. People take up a job or business mainly for sustenance or livelihood. Some people even work for pastime. No matter what the work is, one should meticulously follow his duties in the assigned or chosen work. It is necessary to comply with the rules and regulations of an organization while working. Be it a job or business, one must effectively handle workplace politics, and work with people having different efficiency levels. It is also important to be aware of manipulative tendency or lethargic nature of coworkers. Righteous work ethic is mainly required to purify and stabilize the mind. One must perform his own duties in the best possible way without getting exploited by others. Good work does not mean letting others take you for a ride. In today's age, it is important to choose a job or business which is not rooted in deceiving, looting, swindling or manipulating others. One may earn a lot of wealth with such fraudulent work, but such wealth perturbs the mind and does not lead the seeker to the goal of Self-realization. Choosing meaningful, righteous work for livelihood and doing it diligently is the ideal approach that leads to pure mind and ultimately Self-realization. The seeker must do it as a part of his spiritual pursuit.

Religious rituals (Dharma-Karma, धर्मकर्म)

Many religious rituals such as yajña, pilgrimage, pious observance (Vrata, व्रत), festival celebration and worship are prevalent in Indian society since ancient times. However, most of them have become obsolete in today's age. People conduct them mechanically just for formality, or completely neglect or ridicule them. With changing times and advent of Science and Technology, it has become imperative to renovate the practice of rituals. However, a seeker may not be fully autonomous to change traditional rituals especially due to binding on familial or social level. Even an honest person feels skeptical about religious rituals due to factors such as hypercompetitive world, fast-paced life, turmoil in society, political upheaval, new definitions of well-roundedness, euphoria of the Age of Science, advent of recreational enjoyment, many ways of earning easy wealth, corrupt governance, degrading education system and deliberate mockery of old idealistic ways in society. Many people don't find time for rituals in this dynamic, demanding world. In big cities, this picture is evidently real. People from metro-cities spend their time in doing so-called elite activities such as reading news-papers or magazines, watching TV, browsing internet, using social-media, discussing political issues or partying in clubs. For them religious rituals are stale, outdated and pointless. We should honestly evaluate if this is a 'progress' in real sense. The ambience in small-town or villages is still relatively unpolluted from above factors. People still follow rituals in small towns or villages.

It is good if we can conduct traditionally prescribed rituals. However, if we are unable to do them for some (right or wrong) reason, then it is best to follow the path shown by our enlightened saints. Both Sant Tukārāma and Sant Jñāneśwara have advocated systematic chanting of a Maṅtra as an ideal practice that can replace other religious rituals. Chanting can be done by any person at any time or place. It does not have restrictions like other rituals. Prolonged and consistent chanting eventually leads to pure, calm and stable mind, which is of utmost importance in the path of Self-realization.

Duties (Kartavya-Karma, कर्तव्यकर्म)

Job, business or other professional work must be done for sustenance and livelihood. It is necessary to get monetary returns in professional work. However, personal duties towards family, friends and society should be conducted in a completely selfless manner. For example, a mother and father should take utmost care of their child while raising him, however they should not expect the child to serve them during old-age in return. This is the gist of doing selfless duties. The concept of 'duty' is very vast and expansive. There are many spheres of life where one needs to fulfill his duties. Indian way of life prescribes duties for neighbors, society, parents, teachers, children, nation and ultimately the duty towards self as well. If a person faces conflict between his prescribed duty and traditional religious expectation, he should choose his duty over everything else. This is the central message of Bhagvad-Gītā. (For example, Arjuna was asked to fight the war with his grandfather and Guru, instead of the traditional idea that he should serve them.)

Also, while fulfilling duties for justice, truth and goodness, one should disregard the emotional aspect or traditional values of righteousness. (For example, Lord Kṛṣṇa encouraged Yudhiṣṭhira to 'lie' in the battlefield to enable Arjuna to kill Droṇācārya.) Indian way of life has extensively thought about repaying debts (ṛna, ऋण) on social, familial and national level. People are encouraged to repay their debts in one or the other form. One should not expect appreciation or recognition while repaying these debts. If all familial relations are tied with the bonds of love and duty, there will be harmony on individual, familial as well as social level. Human life will be balanced, coherent and blissful. Performing selfless duties is an imperative factor for purification of mind and Self-realization.

Spiritual pursuit (Adhyātma-Karma, अध्यात्मकर्म)

'Who am I' is the quintessential question of human life. To understand the real Self is the ultimate goal of human birth. Vedānta says that the very nature of every Jīva (embodied soul) is Brahman. To realize Brahman as the real Self, one must follow the spiritual path shown by scriptures and saints.

Sant Jñāneśwara has outlined three specific duties (Satkarma) that every human should follow for enlightenment or Self-realization. The duties are -

- Company of enlightened saints

There is a famous idiom that says – 'Man is known by the company he keeps'. This is true even more in the journey towards Self-realization. Living in the company of enlightened saints is a great spiritual practice. Most people have at least some evil thoughts, wrong impulses or immoral tendencies that are revived in the company of bad people. On the contrary, virtuous, positive and genial thoughts are rekindled in the company of saints. Sant Kabira has famously said – 'A person who is enchained cannot be freed by another person who is himself tied up. For that, the constrained person must seek the help from a completely liberated person.' Similarly, a seeker who is chained by the thought 'I am body' must seek help from saints, who have attained liberation from the bondage of identification with the body. The seeker must honestly introspect, understand and accept his own bad impulses; and then eradicate them gradually in the company of saints. This is an important aspect of Satkarma.

- <u>Knowledge of Yoga</u>

Yoga, in this context, means union of Jīva (individual soul) with Brahman. There are primarily four types of Yoga - **Karmayoga** (path of action), **Bhaktiyoga** (path of devotion), **Dhyānayoga** (path of meditation) and **Jñānayoga** (path of knowledge). A seeker should gain profound knowledge in at least one of these paths from his Guru. He should systematically listen to discourses and reflect on the doctrine of Advaita Vedānta (Śravaṇa, Manana, श्रवण, मनन). This should be followed by deep meditative contemplation (Nididhyāsana, निदिध्यासन), which leads to attainment of Yoga, i.e. Jīva-Brahman union in a real sense. The seeker should be fully composed, clearheaded, steadfast and faithful in the process of Self-realization.

- <u>Serving Sadguru</u>

It is imperative for a seeker to serve his Sadguru with utmost faith and devotion. Serving here is not limited to just physical service or offering material donations. Serving also does not mean offering financial help to Guru by starving one's own family or sidelining one's own responsibilities. Sadguru works mainly for the welfare of his disciples and the society at large. He may face logistical, financial or health-related issues in this work. The seeker should strive to meticulously help and remove these obstacles in his own capacity. Seeker should not fabricate his loyalty or flatter his Guru. The service to Guru is mainly meant to debilitate his own ego and be calm and cheerful. The seeker should nurture detachment from his own material belongings to be able to faithfully serve his Guru. One cannot fully surrender and serve without detachment. However, detachment is a gradual process, it cannot be attained in one night. The seeker should consistently try to maintain disengagement from material world internally, while meticulously carrying out all duties externally.

Execution of Satkarma at each level gradually leads to completely pure and calm mind. Only such pure and calm mind is eligible for Self-realization. After performing Satkarma, the seeker eventually attains liberation or Mokṣa, which is the union of Jīva with Brahman.

THIRD PRAYER

When viciousness is eradicated from mankind, and people consistently perform Satkarma, the world will become a moral, righteous place for living. Moreover, Sant Jñāneśwara wants people to be united by the bonds of genuine love, friendship and companionship for each other. Thus, he seeks to unite the whole society with this third prayer -

भूतां परस्परे पडो । मैत्र जीवाचें ॥ (3rd prayer)

Bhūtāṁ paraspare paḍo | Maitra jīvāceṁ ||

Feelings of jealousy, hatred, envy, violence, defiance and antagonism make it impossible to live happy, blissful and peaceful life. It is important to have affection, sensitivity, empathy, kindness, goodwill and camaraderie among all beings. Jñāneśwara Mahārāja has used the word Bhūta (भूत) in a very broad, all-inclusive manner. It encompasses the 5 great elements (PañcaMahābhūta, पंचमहाभूत), insentient objects and all other sentient beings such as birds, insects etc. The five great elements of earth, water, fire, wind and space should coexist peacefully and be friendly towards all beings. There should be perfect harmony and equilibrium amongst all elements of the nature.

Sant Jñāneśwara, prays to his Guru, 'May the lightning not crack down on trees, houses and animals. May the severe storm not destroy trees, plants, flowers and injure any living being. May the raging fire not burn forests, cities, houses and castles. May the fire grace all living beings by being helpful for cooking and digesting food. May it rain abundantly and let there be no droughts or floods. May the earth grow plentiful trees, fruits and grains. May all animals be useful to humans and may all humans treat them kindly. May humans not be greedy about eating meat prepared by killing animals. May all humans nurture benevolent attitude towards animals, not exploit them commercially, and genuinely try to save them from being killed. May there be genuine cordiality and connectedness in all human relations such as father-son, brother-sister, teacher-student, master-servant, national-foreigner, etc.'

The wish expressed by Sant Jñāneśwara here is in-fact a matter of grave thinking in India today. There is evidently a great conflict, dispute and hostility between human beings based on differences in Religion, caste, political parties, groups, unions, federations, chambers and governance. There is no regard for Sant Jñāneśwara's sublime wish in the society today. Religious feuds and tensions are likely becoming new social norms. There is a deliberate attempt to create tiffs and controversies between different castes for political progress or financial gains. Such news is given prominent coverage by media channels and social media platforms. However, it is totally up to people to study the basics of their own Religion and implement the accurate religious guidelines in daily life. The highly evolved wish of Sant Jñāneśwara cannot be fulfilled without specific effort from every person or seeker at his own level. When the external showcasing part of a Religion becomes dominant, the core inner message of the Religion takes a backseat and gets hidden. Today, the external rituals are evidently being glorified and used for creating hostility and animosity, while the core message of a Religion exists just for namesake.

The situation can be changed only if people take refuge in the texts of saints, and study treatises such as Bhagvad-Gītā or Jñāneśwarī with sincere intentions. Saintly texts can help bring intrinsic change in the mindset of all people. As a result of studying saintly texts, people will gradually behave in a friendly manner with all other living beings. If such harmony and goodwill is indeed developed, there will be no place for conflicts, feuds, revenge, jealousy or hatred in mankind. Protests, turmoil, rallies, riots and processions will gradually diminish from the society. There will be no trace of lawless, antisocial elements, tyrannical political systems and raging wars between nations. The social, economic, political and cultural picture of the world will change completely. Beauty, peace and Bliss will prevail everywhere in the Universe.

FOURTH PRAYER

The third verse in Pasāyadāna has three prayers. The verse is -

दुरितांचे तिमिर जावो । विश्व स्वधर्मसूर्ये पाहो ।
जो जे वांछील तो तें लाहो । प्राणिजात ॥ ३ ॥

Duritāñce timira jāvo / Viśva svadharmasūryeṁ pāho /
Jo je vāñchīla to teṁ lāho / Prāṇijāta // 3 //

- 'May the darkness of sins go away. May the sun of Swadharma (स्वधर्म, Duty-Based Religion) rise on the Universe. May everyone attain what he aspires for.'

Development or debacle of a society depends on virtuous and sinful actions that take place in it. Unless sinful actions are eradicated, social development is not possible. Hence, Jñāneśwara Mahārāja prays for this fourth blessing from his Guru.

दुरितांचे तिमिर जावो । (4th prayer)

Duritāñce timira jāvo /

- 'May the darkness of sins (bad actions) vanish completely from this world.'

People who succumb to sinful behavior do it for their pleasure, just like virtuous people. All actions, good or bad, are ultimately for one's own happiness. However, we need to analyze and understand the concept of real happiness with the help of Vedānta and treatises like Jñāneśwarī. It is impossible for the darkness of sins to go away until we understand where the source of real happiness lies. The systems of Religion, righteousness, law and order, and judiciary regulations have evidently proved to be feeble in the last century. Without the influence of these systems, people still need to learn how to behave appropriately in a regulated and disciplined manner.

It is difficult to discriminate between virtuous and sinful actions in today's age. These definitions change with time, place or circumstances. Hence, Lord Kṛṣṇa says in Bhagvad-Gītā -

तस्माच्छास्त्रं प्रमाणं ते कार्याकार्य व्यवस्थितौ ।

Tasmācchāstraṁ pramāṇaṁ te kāryākārya-vyavasthitau |

- 'Scriptures are the ultimate authoritative texts to discriminate between virtuous and sinful actions.'

Scriptures and saintly texts are created by enlightened, visionary sages, who have absolutely no selfish considerations. Hence, they can guide the mankind in the right direction. Actions, which are recommended by scriptures and saints can be definitively called as 'Religion (धर्म)' or 'virtuous actions'. Actions, which are prohibited by scriptures and saints can be definitively called as 'sins' or 'bad actions'.

Whatever is observed by a large number of people, may not necessarily be 'Religion'. Many people eat meat and drink wine, but that doesn't qualify those actions as being religious. Whatever is shunned by many people may not necessarily be 'sin'. Many people do not love or believe in the God. However, this lack of love is not sin. Religion and sin cannot be defined according to the behavior of masses. But scriptures and saintly texts give a definitive and valuable guidance in this regard, which can be followed everywhere, at all times.

Sinful actions can be performed on two levels.

1. Sinful Actions on Individual Level

These can be of two kinds -

- Hurting others:

There is a famous Sanskrit verse -

परोपकारः पुण्याय । पापाय परपीडनम् ॥

Paropakārah puṇyāya / Pāpāya parapīḍanam //

- 'To help others is a virtue, to hurt others is a sin.'

As readers of Jñāneśwarī and seekers of liberation, it is our responsibility to maintain thoughtful restraint on our own speech and expressions. Verbal wounds are sometime more damaging than physical wounds. Hurting others ultimately brings distress to ourselves. Our mind gets perturbed when we exhibit insensitive behavior. It is not possible to reach the ultimate stage of Self-realization with such disturbed mind. Hence, we should strictly avoid unkind, harmful behavior towards other people.

- <u>Defaming, Greediness and Lustfulness</u>

(Paranindā, Paradhana, Parastrī; परनिंदा, परधन, परस्त्री)

Sant Tukārāma has listed these three primary sins for a seeker. Bad-mouthing others or gossiping behind their back is a total waste of time. It does not bring about any change in the person whom we are defaming. Craving for others' wealth is just a form of daydreaming, which does not change the situation in any practical manner. Being lustful for men or women (other than own spouse) is a sin that only disturbs personal life as well as social harmony. These traits bring great agitation to the mind. They keep us away from our own spiritual pursuit. Pure, Supreme Bliss of Ātman cannot be realized when mind is engaged and disrupted due to these sinful thoughts. We can strive to keep away from these traits at our own level to eradicate the darkness of sins from the society.

2. Sinful Actions on Social level

Sant Jñāneśwara has expressed a wish that sinful actions be completely removed from this world. Many actions such as feuds, brawls and controversies are performed collectively at social level. It may not be possible for one single individual to stop or restrain such contentious situations. However, each one of us can surely try to act or fight injustice according to our own capacity and strength. Taking help of Social Media Platforms such as Facebook, Twitter are great ways to raise one's own voice against wrongdoing in today's age. However, we need to be aware of our own limitations while doing so. If everyone can do his own bit to stop social, collective ruckus, it can progressively lead us towards fulfilling the wish expressed by Sant Jñāneśwara.

It is evident that a sinner suffers miseries in all the three worlds (Swarga, Bhū, Pātāla; स्वर्ग, भू, पाताळ). Lord Kṛṣṇa says in Bhagvad-Gītā (4.31) – 'One who cannot perform good actions in this life, is bound to fail in the life after death.' A sinner usually feels great distress and agitation after doing sinful actions. The disturbed mind in present life is much more harmful than the posthumous punishment of sinful behavior (such as going to hell, etc.). We should consciously strive to avoid any behavior that brings distress to mind as it blocks our own progress towards Self-realization. One sin inevitably leads to another sin and forms a chain. The sinner suffers misery and poverty as a result. If a society is collectively inclined towards sinful behavior, it invites droughts, floods, earthquakes, hailstorms and contagious diseases. We should carefully think about instant repercussions of sinful behavior and stop our own downfall.

The sins of rulers and leaders are much more destructive than those of ordinary people. Sinful rulers lead to anarchy and collapse of political, commercial, administrative and social systems. Ācārya Kamandaka has listed twelve sins, from which the kings, rulers, ministers and leaders should keep themselves away.

1) To be harsh and dismissive to a needy person or a 'life and death' issue.
2) To create and enforce brutal, tyrannical laws
3) Grafting, accepting bribes
4) Consumption of alcohol or narcotics
5) Infidelity, marital disloyalty
6) Gambling, wasting time on playing cards, etc.
7) Hunting animals, birds, etc.
8) To be lazy, lethargic or disinterested in one's own work and duties.
9) Not being open, transparent with anyone.
10) To be conceited and boastful of own position, power or knowledge.
11) To be careless, lenient, inattentive and negligent in own work, misplace crucial official documents, allow encroachment by enemies or breach of national security.
12) To be hostile towards learned, noble, courteous, honorable, poor, feeble or miserable people and punish them harshly.

These sinful acts by rulers result in complete destruction of the society or the nation. Rulers should be aware of the power of the ultimate Supreme Ruler, i.e. the God (Īśvara). Lord Kṛṣṇa says -

गतिर्भर्ता प्रभुः साक्षी निवासः शरणं सुहृत् ।
प्रभवः प्रलयः स्थानं निधानं बीजमव्ययम् ॥ (9.18)

Gatirbhartā prabhuḥ sākṣī nivāsaḥ śaraṇaṁ suhṛt |
Prabhavaḥ pralayaḥ sthānaṁ nidhānaṁ bījamavyayam ||

- 'The entire Universe is ultimately ruled and governed by the God'.

- Human rulers should know that Ātman is the only one Supreme, Eternal Truth. It is the real nature of the Self. The physical body is perishable, but Ātman is perpetual. It transcends the three times of past, present and future. Jīva (embodied soul) is bound by his past actions (Karma, कर्म). Jīva is rewarded or punished in his present life as a result of his own Karma in past lives. This is called as Ānvīkṣikī Vidyā (आन्वीक्षिकी विद्या, Spiritual Knowledge).
- Rulers should have comprehensive knowledge of geography, sociology, Religion and the system of rebirth. They should be aware of the influence of changing times. They should have accurate understanding of the teachings of Vedas and keep utmost faith in Sadguru and scriptures. They should acquire this knowledge with the help of direct perception, logic and the teachings of Vedas. This skill is called as Trayī Vidyā (त्रयी विद्या, Threefold Knowledge).
- Rulers should encourage farming, entrepreneurship, trading, veterinary sciences and lead their citizens to commercial progress. This skill is called as Vārtā Vidyā (वार्ता विद्या, Governing Knowledge).
- Rulers should create constitution, statutes and regulations, to establish and stabilize the above three articles of knowledge. This skill is called as Daṇḍanīti Vidyā (दंडनीति विद्या, Judiciary Knowledge).

Rulers should create laws and statutes based on the following important principles -

- Īśvara has created this Universe. He governs it based on His own laws and system.
- The world is made up of three Guṇas - Sattva, Rajas and Tamas. The enormous disparity in the world is the result of various combinations of the three Guṇas. (Sattva - inclined towards peace, purity and honesty, Rajas - inclined towards activity, splendor and selfishness, Tamas - inclined towards laziness and wickedness)
- The Law of Karma - every human being experiences joys or sorrows as result of his own past actions.
- Human beings are innately different from each other. Their intrinsic desires along with cultural, occupational, intellectual, social and family influences cause these differences.
- Man is a social animal.
- Ideal human life is based on four pillars -
    1. Dharma - righteous thinking and performing duties towards self and the world with utmost sincerity
    2. Artha - material progress
    3. Kāma - sensual desires
    4. Mokṣa - Self-realization

Every ruler, big or small, should have comprehensive knowledge about these principles. In case he is unable to learn himself, he should seek to learn from the insightful and discerning people in the field. Lord Rāma learnt the knowledge from his Guru Vasiṣṭha ṛṣi, Lord Kṛṣṇa learnt from Sandipanī Munī and King Śivājī learnt from Sant Tukārāma and Sant Rāmdāsa. Hence, there was no darkness of sins and immoral behavior in their kingdoms.

Sant Jñāneśwara has made this all-embracing request for 'removal of sinful actions' to his Guru for the betterment of entire humanity. The sins must vanish at all levels - individual, society and the world. Only then true peace and Bliss will prevail everywhere. For that, each one of us must strive to eliminate sinful actions, tendencies in our own lives.

FIFTH PRAYER

When tendency for sinful actions vanishes, we must replace it with noble actions. Man cannot stay without action even for a second. There is indeed no point in performing worthless or malicious actions. It is important to act in a positive, virtuous manner. Hence, Sant Jñāneśwara prays for the fifth blessing -

विश्व स्वधर्मसूर्यें पाहो । (5th prayer)

Viśva svadharmasūryeṁ pāho |

- 'May the sun of Swadharma (Duty-Based Religion, स्वधर्म) enlighten the Universe.'

The word Dharma traditionally stands for Religion. Swadharma indicates performing actions or duties in a sincere and scrupulous manner. The word Swadharma has very wide implications. It does not merely indicate religious sects such as Hinduism, Islam or Christianity. Religion is only a small facet or part of it.

The word 'Swadharma' in this verse has been explained beautifully by Lord Kṛṣṇa in Bhagvad-Gītā -

स्वे स्वे कर्मण्यभिरतः संसिद्धिं लभते नरः ॥ (18.45)

Sve sve karmaṇyabhirataḥ saṁsiddhiṁ labhate naraḥ ||

Swadharma, here, means executing one's own duties towards family, society, nation and humanity, with utmost devotion and sincerity. These duties are peculiar to only human beings. The lower animals are aware of just the bare necessities of existence such as food, clothing, shelter, sleep, fear, etc. Only human beings can perform actions beyond fulfilling the basic needs of life. Duties were determined based on Āśrama and Varṇa in ancient days in India, but that system is completely obsolete now. In today's age, the duties are purely based on the work that is assigned to or accepted by a person. A person who is negligent, lethargic, careless or a mere show-off should be considered as being irreligious in today's age. Duties invariably include actions that one may like or dislike. However, they need to be performed meticulously in any case. The principle that 'Work is Worship' is of utmost importance.

Every person is expected to perform duties on two levels-

1. Duties on Personal Level

Everyone has duties towards himself as well as immediate family members. Personal duties involve two aspects – materialistic progress and spiritual progress (**Abhyudaya** and **Niḥśreyasa** – अभ्युदय, निःश्रेयस). These should go together as prescribed by Bhagvad-Gītā and Vedānta. We should strive to live prosperous material life. At the same time, it is important to understand the real nature of the Self with the help of ancient Indian scriptures such as Upaniṣads, Bhagvad-Gītā and saintly texts.

Duties towards family involve helping and caring for them in a loving and selfless manner.

- Son or daughter - To take good care of parents and attend to their medical needs during old-age.
- Father - To ensure good upbringing and righteous behavior of his children. He should ensure that his children get useful education, and stay away from addictions, bad habits and vices.
- Mother - To nourish and feed her child and take care of the overall health and well-being of the child.
- Wife - To be devoted to her husband and help him perform his duties.
- Husband - To be devoted to wife and encourage her to feel involved in execution of duties, earning livelihood, carnal pleasures and Self-realization.
- Brother or Sister - Help and support each other in times of need.

Indian scriptures like Rāmāyaṇa and Mahābhārata offer extraordinary examples to guide us in this regard. Lord Rāma immediately followed the wish of his father Daśaratha, left his kingdom and stayed in the forest. Sītā left the comforts and luxuries of royal palace to accompany her husband Rāma for 14 years. Laxman left his own wife and family to serve his elder brother in forest. All 5 Pāṇḍavas married Draupadī only to follow the order of their mother Kuntī. Indian culture shows how duties towards family members can be performed in the most sublime manner. It is clearly not possible to literally follow these examples in today's age. However, we can surely perform duties with genuine love and devotion for our relatives to fulfill the wish expressed by Sant Jñāneśwara in Pasāyadāna.

2. Duties on Social Level

The society is mainly sustained by people in these four professions -

1. Knowledge - To acquire knowledge in various fields, enhance the knowledge and evolve the expertise; teach to others and work for intellectual upliftment of the society.
2. Governance and Protection - To govern the people with law, rules and regulation; protect the society from evil forces, crooks; and protect the nation from foreign invaders.
3. Business and Agriculture - To cultivate land, run various industries and professions for commercial advancement and material progress of the society.
4. Service - To assist people from all three above categories in their respective fields.

Most people work in one of these four categories. To fulfill the noble wish of Sant Jñāneśwara, each one of us must meticulously execute duties in our own field. Each profession comes with its own set advantages and disadvantages. We should embrace the work with all its challenges and strive to excel in it.

The field of knowledge is divided into 2 categories. They are -

Scientific Knowledge (Vijñāna, विज्ञान)

This includes knowledge pertaining to everyday life such as Technology, Commerce, Arts, Sports, Medicine etc. We should invest in learning new upcoming branches of knowledge and progress in our own field.

Spiritual Knowledge (Jñāna, ज्ञान)

This involves living life for spiritual, moral, religious and righteous upliftment of the society.

There are evidently many fields of knowledge today. Each field has its own set of ups and downs. A discerning person may wonder, 'Which one is the best and the highest knowledge?'. Lord Kṛṣṇa has answered this question in Bhagvad-Gītā -

अध्यात्मविद्या विद्यानां ।

Adhyātmavidyā-Vidyānām |

- 'Spiritual Knowledge (about the real Self or Brahman) is the highest form of knowledge.'

There is a reason why Gītā propounds the Knowledge of Brahman (Self) as the highest knowledge. All other fields offer only a limited, transient happiness to human beings. For example, a builder (civil engineer) may build a spectacular house for a person. An expert doctor may eradicate grave disease and make a person healthy. However, good health and good house do not guarantee

Eternal, Pure Bliss to any person. There are many more factors that are needed for happy, joyous and content life. No single profession can offer it to human beings. Only the Knowledge of Brahman can fill the human life with Pure, Eternal Bliss. Hence, people who lead others on the path of Self-realization (knowledge that the real Self is Brahman), in-turn live the most meaningful life themselves.

In short, everyone should aspire to fulfill his duties both on personal and social level in the finest manner.

Conflict between duties

Many times, a person is faced with a conflict to choose between two important duties that need to be done at the same time. For example, teaching a class of students vs. taking care of a sick relative at home; or attending patients in hospital vs. feeding a hungry child at home etc. People feel tormented when they are faced with such conflicting duties.

Scriptures such as Rāmāyaṇa and Mahābhārata offer insightful examples in this regard. Lord Rāma gave preference to his duty as a ruling king and left his wife Sītā in forest, as was the demand of the situation at that time. He devalued his duty as a husband and chose to serve people of his kingdom. Many people in today's age find this decision controversial. They even accuse Lord Rāma of being greedy for ruling power and ignoring his wife. However, careful study of original Vālmīki

Rāmāyaṇa reveals that Lord Rāma slept on the bed of dry grass before the day of his scheduled coronation. He followed the wish of his father and immediately left the kingdom on the day of his coronation. Also, when he came back to the kingdom after 14 years, he first checked goodwill of his younger brother Bharata and only then re-entered the palace. These incidents clearly testify the fact that there was not even a tinge of greediness for ruling power in Lord Rāma's mind. However, when he had to choose between serving people and taking care of wife, he chose to serve people. There are similar stories in Mahābhārata when Lord Kṛṣṇa advised Pāṇḍavas to disregard the traditional guidelines of Religion and righteousness to ensure that evil people in society are defeated. (Yudhiṣṭhira was asked to lie with Droṇācārya, Bhīma was asked to break the rules of war while fighting with Duryodhana, Arjuna was asked to take help of Śikhaṇḍī to defeat Bhīṣma, etc.)

All these stories testify the fact that duties towards society (or masses) should be deemed more important than one's personal duties towards self or family. When one is faced with a more sublime or inclusive goal, the duties pertaining to smaller, individual goals should naturally take a back-seat. These are clear guidelines from our own scriptures and ancestors.

Purpose of Duty-Based Religion (Swadharma, स्वधर्म)

We must reflect on why there is such an emphasis on performing duties in the finest manner. Every action is associated with a result. One may see the result immediately after performing action, or sometime later in future. Future means 'future time in current birth' or 'future births'. Action and its future results have a definite '**Cause and Effect**' relationship (KāryaKāraṇa Bhāva, कार्यकारण भाव). The actions performed in human birth determine the course of next birth or future times. Sant Jñāneśwara says, 'sinful actions in this birth give hell or beastly life in future. Virtuous and selfish actions lead to heaven or divine life in future. Noble and selfless actions purify the mind, and lead to Self-realization.' This is called as the '**Law of Karma**'.

It is difficult to understand and accept this law, since human thinking is limited to what can be seen, proved or experienced by five senses. Actions which yield results in the same birth can be possibly comprehended by humans. But it is difficult to comprehend how actions performed in this birth give results in the next birth.

In everyday life, it is commonly seen that we do not always get immediate results of actions. After sowing seeds, it takes time for crops to grow and give grains. Similarly, (some) actions that we perform in this birth germinate and give appropriate (good or bad) fruits only in future births. We can also discern that some inexplicable circumstances in current life must be the result of actions from our past births. However, the discussion of rebirth or past birth evokes almost immediate cynicism, skepticism, and sarcasm at all intellectual levels. Many people turn atheists when they stumble at this stage. However, this happens because the so-called brilliant intellect is incapable of discerning very subtle topics of nature. Most people follow the beaten, routine and traditional path of life. Those who try to delve into the finer, deeper, subtler and extra-sensory facts are very few, because such facts are inconsequential in everyday life. The 'Law of Karma' is a deep and subtle principle. The death of one body and the gap of many years between two births make it impossible to have direct, first-hand knowledge about it. The intellect, however brilliant in physical Sciences, is incapable of discerning the 'Cause and Effect' relationship between action and its results.

The system of cycling through multiple births and the Law of Karma, are very well explained in Vedas. The verses in Vedas were revealed to Ṛṣis in ancient India when they were deeply meditating. These verses explain facts of life, which are not man-made. Ṛṣis experienced these verses through years of patient, resilient and scientific efforts to unite their minds with that of the Universe. The Universal Mind is timeless, ageless, all-pervading and all-knowing.

There are two obvious and logical proofs that testify the possibility of cycling through multiple rebirths. Any newborn baby innately knows how to sleep, cry, latch his mouth and suck milk from his mother. A baby in crawling stage feels scared of strange surrounding or people. The baby does not need to be trained for these actions. This shows that reflexes such as sucking, fear and crying are inherent in the baby. They are the result of former experiences and imprints from past lives. Many people experience inexplicable, bizarre incidents in their life, which cannot be attributed to any possible, obvious reason in present life. It is only logical to presume that there ought to be some reason for these bizarre incidents that can be traced back to the previous life. The Law of Karma can thus be comprehended by an insightful, perceptive and discerning person.

If everyone follows his or her own duties judiciously, we will never see the darkness of sins, viciousness, infidelity, antagonism, greed, hatred, rivalries and wars. Many suns of Swadharma will rise together and illumine the world with the golden light of purity and auspiciousness.

SIXTH PRAYER

Now Sant Jñāneśwara explains the result of the observance of Swadharma -

जो जे वांछील तो तें लाहो । प्राणिजात ॥ (6th prayer)

Jo je vāñchīla to teṁ lāho | Prāṇijāta ||

- 'May everybody get what he wishes for.'

Sant Jñāneśwara has prayed for a very gracious blessing for the fulfillment of all wishes by everyone in the world. Some people may misinterpret that Sant Jñāneśwara has asked for fulfillment of evil wishes made by malicious people as well, which is clearly incorrect. It is important to understand the spirit of this verse. Every action is invariably tied to a result. One is bound to get results whether one wants them or not. One need not expect the result to be able to get it. Once the mind is conditioned to this system, everyone will be at peace with the results that come his way. The only real meaning here is that people should understand the 'Law of Karma', regulate their actions and not expect specific results of actions.

There is a very delicate relationship between Swadharma (execution of duties) and getting all comforts in life. For example, when a husband and wife both follow Swadharma, the wife meets her husband with love, affection and devotion. Both plunge into raptures of joy. However, a prostitute meets a man in a purely selfish, professional and robotic manner, since it is an enforced relationship.

Similarly, one who follows Swadharma can enjoy his life in a joyful and transparent manner. One who earns money by law-abiding, upright and ethical means, can enjoy his earnings fearlessly. He can lift himself to religious, moral and spiritual heights in life. However, one who earns money through grafting, illegitimate and other unlawful means, readily invites trouble from the law, fellow goons and thugs.

There is one more meaning to this verse. It is surely impractical and impossible that all wishes of every (good or bad) person will be satisfied. We must then reflect on the questions, 'Whose wishes and which wishes may be rightfully satisfied?'. People (seekers) should first work on the prerequisites outlined in Pasāyadāna -

- Eliminate their own evil tendencies
- Perform Satkarmas that lead to purification of mind
- Avoid sinful actions
- Execute their duties with utmost dedication

Only people who have met these conditions are eligible to make wishes (that may be completely fulfilled). Also, the wishes should not be made with selfish or individualistic outlook. There is a famous prayer in Upaniṣads -

> ॐ सर्वे भवन्तु सुखिनः । सर्वे सन्तु निरामयाः ।
> सर्वे भद्राणि पश्यन्तु । मा कश्चित् दुःखभाग् भवेत् ॥
>
> *Om Sarve bhavantu sukhinaḥ / Sarve santu nirāmayāḥ /*
> *Sarve bhadrāṇi paśyantu / Mā kaścid duhkhabhag bhavet /*
> *Om Śantiḥ Śantiḥ Śantiḥ //*
>
> - 'May all become happy, may all be healthy, i.e. free from illness, may all see what is auspicious, and may no one suffer in any way.'

Vedānta encourages us to think beyond the limits of individual, narrow, bounded life. It teaches us to broaden our horizon and wish for everyone's happiness. Such evolved and all-inclusive prayers cannot be found in the literature of any other so-called progressive culture. This verse has implicit connotation that only such broad, holistic and all-encompassing wishes made by worthy, noble people may be fulfilled. It indeed is a gratifying experience to understand and assimilate the real spirit and message of this verse in Pasāyadāna.

SEVENTH PRAYER

There are many religious orders, sects, faiths, doctrines, clans and communities in the world. Why and how will everyone follow the teachings of Vedas? Secondly, the world is full of people with varied tendencies and temperaments. Lord Kṛṣṇa Says in Bhagvad-Gītā -

द्वौ भूतसर्गौ लोकेऽस्मिन्दैव आसुर एव च । (16.6)

Dvau bhūta-sargau loke'asmin daiva āsura eva ca |

- 'There are two kinds of people in the world. One with divine qualities, the other with demoniac qualities.'

Some are virtuous, religious, dutiful, sincere, righteous, peaceful, kind, soft, generous and good-hearted. Some are swindlers, corrupt, deceitful, atheists, heartless, vicious, greedy, selfish and inhumane in nature.

Sant Jñāneśwara keeps this diversity in mind and prays to the God that saints should mingle with all kinds of people. Being pure and selfless themselves, saints have the power to change all sorts of people intrinsically and make them better human beings.

वर्षत सकळमंगळी । ईश्वरनिष्ठांची मांदियाळी ।

अनवरत भूमंडळी । भेटो तया भूतां ॥ ४ ॥ (7th prayer)

Varṣata sakaḻa maṅgaḻī / Īśvaraniṣṭhāṅcī māṅdiyāḻī /

Anavarata bhūmaṅḍaḻī / Bheṭo tayā bhūtāṁ // 4 //

- 'May the entire humanity meet all gracious saints, who incessantly shower the teachings of righteous thinking all over the Universe.'

Sanctity of genuine saints can remove impurity of atheism from the society. They are the authentic, real teachers of mankind. Efforts made by unrighteous people to reform the society are futile and sometimes even dangerous. There is a huge difference between education imparted by experts vs. novice people in the field. Work done by wise and adept people is surely much superior to the one done by incompetent people. Saints are completely selfless in their efforts to uplift and reform the society, hence their efforts are truly auspicious in nature. On the contrary, the social or patriotic work done by greedy, selfish and hurtful people, is neither useful nor commendable in nature. Only saints can bring intrinsic transformation in the society. They can cultivate the faith in Īśvara (God) in the society. They can change the mindset of people and make them follow the path of Swadharma.

This wish expressed by Sant Jñāneśwara cannot surely be fulfilled by anyone other than the omnipotent and omnipresent Īśvara. In these verses Sant Jñāneśwara discusses the real value of saints and the necessity of their presence in the society. There is a verse in Sanskrit that says - **ज्ञानेशो भगवान विष्णुः** (*Jñāneśo Bhagvāna Viṣṇuḥ*), which means only Sant Jñāneśwara can fulfill his own wish (in this case), since he himself is an incarnation of Lord Viṣṇu. He asked for this particular blessing from his Guru Sant Nivṛttināthа just for formality and his Guru granted him the same blessing. Sant Jñāneśwara has wished that this entire Universe be showered with the presence of Īśvara-Niṣṭhā (ईश्वरनिष्ठ) saints.

The word **Īśvara-Niṣṭha** (ईश्वरनिष्ठ) is quite remarkable. Īśvara means **Iśān** (ईशान) or the governor (controller) of the Universe. All living and non-living beings are governed by Īśvara. The Law of Karma states that all human beings should perform work and execute duties to the best of their abilities, however the results of those actions are governed by Īśvara. The word Īśvara-Niṣṭhā means one who willingly accepts the establishment of Īśvara and peacefully embraces every situation in life, after having worked in the best possible manner. There are many people who worship the God with external means such as flowers, lights, sweets, incense, etc. However, internally they feel discontent, restless, angry and frustrated for adverse conditions in their lives. For example, a young person may be inflicted with a disease such as cancer or diabetes even after taking utmost care of his health. Two equally competent doctors or lawyers may get completely different success, fame or money in their professions. A mother who lovingly takes care of her child may in-turn get neglected by him in old-age. All these examples testify the fact that human life is surely governed by Īśvara.

It is the responsibility of a seeker (reader) to understand the real spirit of the word Īśvara-Niṣṭhā, and unconditionally accept the results after having performed his duties in the best possible manner. The world is a hypercompetitive place today. People in every profession feel constant pressure to perform well in their jobs and deliver results. Working people naturally feel stressed due to peer-pressure. Later, they feel dissatisfied for the results that they get, or jealous of others who get better results. Sant Jñāneśwara gives us a fresh new perspective to look at this system. He says that actions should be performed in such exceptional manner that they get noticed and appreciated even by Īśvara.

तैसे आपुलेनी विहिता। उपायो असे न विसंबिता।
ऐसा कीजे की जगन्नाथा। आभारु पडे॥

Taise āpulenī vihitā | Upāyo ase na visambitā |
Aisā kīje kī Jagannāthā | Ābhāru paḍe || (Jñā. 18.910)

- 'Do your work in such excellent, selfless and tireless manner that even Īśvara feels burdened by it.'

There is no thought of abandoning or renouncing actions in the spiritual path. Sant Jñāneśwara encourages us to perform consistent and excellent actions in life. Actions can be performed with a sense of competitiveness and stress to outperform other people (as is prevalent in the society these days). The same actions can be peacefully performed in the finest manner to please Īśvara. Either way, actions get the results only as per the system of Īśvara. However, in the latter case, a person can enjoy his own actions instead of feeling pressured to survive in the competitive world around him.

This is a great approach, where we are motivated to work in a superlative manner, however we are taught to accept the results (good or bad) calmly and happily. It eliminates all negative feelings of selfishness, enmity, envy, indignation and bitterness from mind. Mind becomes gradually pure and stable (Cittaśuddhi and Cittaśānti, चित्तशुद्धि, चित्तशांति). When prescribed duties (towards family, society etc.) are done in exceptional and selfless manner, they turn into beautiful flowers (of Karma). Īśvara bestows his grace on selfless, honest, hard-working people. With his grace, we can naturally progress on the path of spiritual fortune and lead to the ultimate stage of Self-realization.

Sant Jñāneśwara has an implicit wish that we (readers) should assimilate this spirit, mold our own behavior and spread the teaching at our own level. If all people learn to worship God in a steadfast manner, there will surely be goodness and auspiciousness in the society.

Enlightened saints are naturally selfless and nurture unconditional surrender to Īśvara. Hence, Sant Jñāneśwara has expressed a wish that the society be filled with large number of such benevolent saints. They should spread the values of piousness, ethical thinking and righteous behavior in the society; and people should embrace their teachings wholeheartedly. It is up to Īśvara to ensure large number of such saints are born; however, it is up to us to accept and assimilate their teachings.

Non-believer people live in the state of perpetual delusion and ignorance. They are skeptical about their actual duties as well as goals. They are possessed with ego in many different forms. Lord Kṛṣṇa describes such people in these verses of Bhagvad-Gītā -

आढ्योभिजनवानस्मि कोन्योस्ति सदृशो मया । (16.15)

Āḍhyobhijanavān asmi konyosti sadṛśo mayā |

- 'I am the richest man, surrounded by many relatives. There is none so powerful and happy as I am.'

ईश्वरोहमहं भोगी सिद्धोहं बलवान्सुखी । (16.14)

Iśvarohamahaṃ bhogī siddhohaṃ balavānsukhī |

- 'I am the Lord of everything. I am the enjoyer. I am happy and the powerful dictator.'

With such manifestations of the ego, these people become arrogant and disdainful. They continue being insolent until they are met with a rude jolt that shakes their very belief and existence. If the ruler is a non-believer, he ruins the nation. If major portion of the society is not following Swadharma, it will destroy itself. When a member or head of the family is a non-believer, he brings misfortune to himself or the family.

It must be conceded that there will be some robbers, swindlers and vicious, brutal, wicked people in the society. But they cannot ruin the community, society or nation as a whole. They may only destroy themselves. But when rulers, leaders and politicians emerge from groups of vicious people, maliciousness percolates to all layers of the society, and it ruins the entire nation. With this wide perspective, Sant Jñāneśwara has asked for close contact of the noble, kindhearted saints with entire humanity.

The primary teaching imparted by saints is - 'Śrutis (Upaniṣads / Vedas) are the directives of the God. It is the highest duty of a man to follow them. Follower of Śrutis will surely get material as well as spiritual fulfillment in life.'

The rationale for this teaching can be easily seen and verified. Today, the societies and nations are being governed mainly by the laws of judicial system. However, Vedas (Śrutis) are much more authoritative than (man-made) laws. This is because -

- The laws are framed by human intellect, which is prone to prejudices, and errors of foresight and judgement. Human intellect (Buddhi, बुद्धि) is tainted with 4 types of faults: illusion, blunder, imperfect senses and excessive greed (Bhrama, Pramāda, Karaṇāpāṭava, Vipralipsā - भ्रम, प्रमाद, करणापाटव, विप्रलिप्सा). The law-making process made by error-prone human intellect is as old as human race, and yet it is incomplete, imperfect and always evolving to date.

- The frequent changes in the law-system are vigorously defended by leaders and law-makers. Hence, there is no provision for sustenance of firm and stable human values in the law.
- The enforcement of laws also has its own limitations. The process of proving breach of law is complicated and the law always reveals itself after its breach.
- Law does not have any bearing on virtuous or sinful actions. There is no law that prescribes that food must be given to poor beggars or disabled people. But if a generous person gives it, he is being 'virtuous' as per the scriptures. The law does not forbid eating food prepared by killing animals. However, killing animals, especially cows, and eating their meat is a 'sin' as per the scriptures. Hence, law cannot provide definitive guidance to discriminate between 'virtuous' (religious) and 'sinful' (irreligious) actions to the society.

Vedas, on the other hand, are not written manually. They are manifested from the divine brilliant intellect (**Ṛtambharā Prajñā**, ऋतंभरा प्रज्ञा) of various Ṛṣis and sages. **Ṛta** means **Satya** or the transcendental truth. Ṛṣis from ancient India were known to have pure, unadulterated and truthful mind. The verses of Vedas were heard by Ṛṣis (ṣruta, श्रुत) when they were deeply meditating. Since these words are manifested from their 'divine intellect', they are devoid of the four faults of human intellect mentioned above. Swadharma (set of duties) as explained by Vedas, governs the human mind with righteousness. So, people intrinsically stay away from crimes or vicious deeds. If someone still executes a crime, he is punished in this or next birth by the God. There is no question of amendment of principles preached by Vedas.

Vedas are evidently more authentic than man-made laws. The maker of Vedas (the God) is greater than Vedas. However, genuine saints are greater than both the God and Vedas, because they can explain Vedas and experience the God. Saints explain the knowledge outlined in Vedas very well to one and all.

Law is ultimately man-made; hence it is subject to selfishness, partisanship, human failings and other narrow-minded considerations.

The human beings can be classified in five grades of inclinations or attitudes. We take, for example, an 'inclination to steal'.

Grade-1: These are the people who have no faith in Vedas, Religion, saints or the God, but generally scared of the law. Such people find stealing much easier than working hard and earning money. They are skillful thieves who take utmost care while stealing money. They face imprisonment or share the loot with the police, if caught while stealing. They are willing to pay crafty lawyers and even bribe the judges if needed. They look forward to living a reputable life after being released and even seek leadership in the society. Most rogues, swindlers, criminals and vicious people fall in this category.

Grade-2: Leading professionals, industrialists or renowned businessmen in the society are quite law-abiding in nature. People in this category might take advantage of loop-holes in the law and try to circumvent it. They may even influence the law-making process to suit their needs. They try to be in the good books of prominent government officials, ministers and politicians. Such people are selfish, astute and shrewd in nature. In any case, they try to protect their wealth and reputation.

Grade-3: These are the people, who honestly feel that stealing in any form is a sin and against the teachings of Vedas and saints. They believe that flouting these teachings will lead to punishment in this or the next life. These are the God loving and self-disciplined people.

Grade-4: Seekers and those who desire liberation (Mokṣa, मोक्ष) believe that material pursuits of wealth, power, fame etc. are meaningless. They think it is better to follow Swadharma (स्वधर्म, Duty-Based Religion) in a selfless manner, earn blessings of the God, surrender to Sadguru and reach the stage of Self-realization in human life.

Grade-5: Sages, seers and saints perform noble, selfless duties of helping others to make their lives peaceful and blissful. Sant Jñāneśwara, Kabira, Tulsidāsa etc. fall in this category.

There are increasingly more sublime and elevated tendencies of human beings as mentioned above. Everyone is equal under the law, but these five classes are inevitably found in all human societies of the world. Saints can bring about change in the first and second categories of people, and they guide the rest of the grades to their ultimate goal. They reform the people in society in three different ways.

1) If a person is an absolute evil, vicious or deceptive, saints daze him with some inconceivable miracle, and show him the power of God. This makes him believe in the existence of the God and ultimately love him. When a buffalo was being lashed by a whip by some nasty people, Sant Jñāneśwara showed the marks of the whip on his own back and brought about complete change in the mind of those cynic people.
2) The sublime, virtuous and selfless behavior of saints impresses the minds of unethical, sinful people. Sant Nārada, who was the epitome of purity and devotion, influenced Vālya, a highway dacoit. He converted Vālya into sage Vālmīki, who later wrote the very famous epic of Rāmāyaṇa.
3) Saints convince the intellectual atheists or sceptics with constructive debates and arguments. Sant Śaṅkarācārya convinced Maṇḍana Miśrā by defeating him in a debate using pure logic and reasoning. Sant

Tukārāma convinced Rāmeśwara Bhatta with his own righteous thoughts and conduct.

Thus, saints establish the importance of Swadharma (Duty-Based Religion) in the society using different techniques and strategies. For the cohesive balance and stability of a society or nation, it is important that there is belief in the existence of the God. It is necessary that people nurture genuine faith in Īśvara, and His power to govern the Universe based on good and bad deeds. Only then there will be religious, social and political equilibrium in the society.

ADDENDUM TO THE SEVENTH PRAYER

It is indeed a great wish that entire mankind should come in touch with kindhearted saints. However, meeting saints is futile if people ridicule their teachings as backward, orthodox, obsolete, pointless or impractical. It is important that saints are accepted, revered and loved by the society. People should be convinced that their teachings lead to the ultimate benefit and welfare of mankind. Sant Jñāneśwara now describes saints in these verses -

चलां कल्पतरूंचे आरव । चेतना चिंतामणींचें गाव ।
बोलते जे अर्णव । पीयूषाचे ॥ ५ ॥
चंद्रमें जे अलांछन । मार्तंड जे तापहीन ।
ते सर्वांही सदा सज्जन । सोयरे होतु ॥ ६ ॥

Calāṁ kalpatarūṅce ārava |
Cetanā ciṅtāmaṇīṅceṁ gāva |
Bolate je arṇava | Pīyūṣhāce || 5 ||
Caṅdrame je alāṅchana | Mārtaṅḍa je tāpahīna |
Te sarvāṅhī sadā sajjana | Soyare hotu || 6 ||

He has used 5 different metaphors (Kalpataru, Cintāmaṇi, Ocean, Moon, Sun) to describe the primacy of saints for the progress of the mankind. However, each of these metaphors has some shortcoming. Sant

Jñāneśwara beautifully describes the grandeur, brilliance and timelessness of saints, which transcends these metaphors.

Kalpataru:

There is a popular legend that Kalpataru tree fulfills all wishes made by people who sit beneath it. Sant Jñāneśwara says that saints are like gardens of Kalpataru trees, which are laden with fruits and flowers of teachings and blessings. These gardens are not stationary, but they are moving from place to place. This verse says that saints evidently do not meditate in a secluded place but move about in the society with genuine concern to uplift people. They touch people from all strata of the society. They understand the miseries, flaws, weak spots and shortcomings of everyone and guide them accordingly. They are pious like river Gaṅgā, which flows, nourishes and purifies everything that it touches. They help people fulfill their aspirations in a righteous and dutiful manner.

People who take refuge of the company of saints, notice that their desires are gradually diminished and eradicated completely. Mind becomes pure, quiet, calm and composed. 'Fulfilling the desires' in this case means that desires don't even arise in the mind when we live life according to the guidance of saintly texts. Desires can manifest in many forms such as hope, wish, expectation, aspiration, craving, attachment, day-dreams and greed etc. Mind remains in a disturbed and agitated condition so long as desires are present in it. Taittirīya Upaniṣad has described the ladder of increasing happiness. It has a verse that says -

> श्रोत्रियस्य अकामहतस्य ।
>
> *Śrotriyasya Akāmahatasya* |
>
> - 'One who realizes Brahman and stays detached from desires can experience Pure, Supreme Bliss.'

The company of saints (and their teachings) gradually eradicates all desires and calms the mind; hence they 'fulfill all desires' in true sense.

Indian philosophy prescribes ideal life based on fulfillment of the 'fourfold achievements' (The Caturvidha Puruṣārtha) - **Dharma, Artha, Kāma** and **Mokṣa**. If Dharma (Religion) is followed in a selfish or superficial manner, or just for showoff, it is Adharma (irreligion). If Artha is practiced with dishonesty, it is Adharma. Kāma, if not enjoyed according to Dharma, it is reduced to debauchery. Mokṣa, if not understood, practiced and realized according to scriptures, it is frivolousness. Saints see to it that everyone follows his duties (Dharma) as prescribed by Vedas, and everyone luxuriates in Pure Bliss.

Cintāmaṇi:

Cintāmaṇi is a precious stone that is believed to eradicate all worries and fulfill all wishes of its owner. It is not commonly available in this Universe. Jñāneśwara Mahārāja says that saints are like the township built from Chiṅtāmaṇis, only they are sentient in nature. Saints themselves approach people, who are not perceptive enough to seek saintly company. For seekers, saints guide them throughout their journey towards Self-realization. All genuine queries are answered properly and put to rest by saints. The afflictions of three types, i.e. Ādhyātmika, Ādhibhautika, and Ādhidaivika Tāpa are eradicated in the company of saints. The Vedas are presiding main deities of this township of saints. Swadharma (performing duties), chanting, devotion, detachment, renunciation and liberation are accurately explained, preached, practiced and realized in this exclusive township.

Sant Jñāneśwara has used the metaphor of Cintāmaṇi, since all worries disappear when one takes shelter in the company of saints. Mind does not cling to any concern or fear when one learns to live life as per the teachings of saints; it eventually dissolves in the Pure Bliss of Ātman.

Ocean:

Saints are oceans of nectar. A regular ocean may just roar loudly but that sound is meaningless. Plus, the ocean water is salty and cannot be consumed. Saints however, speak a language, which is sweeter than nectar and their teachings are deeper than the ocean. They impart their message in soft yet profound words. The impact of their pleasant words and mellifluous voice is such that the seeker eventually revels in the Pure Bliss of Brahman. Saints gently peel the masking of words, uncover their deep meanings and convey them to the seekers. They explain the hidden, not-so obvious meanings of all intricate words in Vedānta and ensure that seekers reach the stage of Self-realization. Brahman is the nectar of Pure Bliss. Words that escort the seeker towards realization of Brahman are nectar in themselves too. Saints are like oceans of these profound, gratifying words. Seekers revel in their teachings and intellectuals are convinced by their poignant discourses.

Moon:

The moon is calming but it has blemishes. Saints are like the luminous moon without blemishes. Their presence is highly soothing and comforting. They appease seekers with their rays of teachings. Their lives are sinless, and their conduct is faultless. People bow their heads in reverence and seek fulfillment of their own lives by following the teachings of saints. The moon grows and diminishes in size. However, Saints are personification of Brahman, which is constant and eternal. So, they do not change in essence and continue to exist in the form of their teachings.

Sun:

Saints are like the sun without scorching heat. They illumine seekers with the light of the knowledge of Brahman. With their radiant light, they can wipe out the illusion that the surrounding world is real. They enlighten all genuine and committed seekers with Pure Knowledge of Brahman and remove darkness of ignorance from lives of others.

Sant Jñāneśwara expresses a noble wish that people in society love such saints, serve them and have unqualified faith in their teachings for their own liberation. Their biographies are timeless and inspirational to one and all. There are many enlightened people who stay in caves, mountains, or other remote places. However, they are not useful for the upliftment of ordinary people. Hence, Sant Jñāneśwara wishes for presence of saints who can mingle with the society and help bring intrinsic reforms in the state of the society. He says that such saints should guide all people in every era. His wish encompasses all people irrespective of their gender, age, Religion, caste, mindset and social, educational or economic background.

EIGHTH PRAYER

To lead the entire world towards its welfare, Sant Jñāneśwara now outlines actions that need to be followed by all people, and the results of those actions.

> किंबहुना सर्व सुखी । पूर्ण होऊनि तिहीं लोकी ।
> भजिजो आदिपुरुखी । अखंडित ॥ ७ ॥
>
> *Kiṁbahunā sarva sukhī | Pūrṇa hoūni tinhīṁ lokī |*
> *Bhajijo Ādipurukhī | Akhaṇḍita || 7 ||*
>
> - 'People from all three worlds (earth, heaven and infernal world), should worship the Universal God for achieving happiness on all fronts.' (8th prayer)

Ādi means the most primeval principle. The word Ādipurukh (Ādipuruṣa) in this verse stands for the God and it indicates two meanings -

- Brahman - Brahman means (Pure) Existence, Consciousness, Bliss (Sat, Cit, Ananda). Upaniṣads say that the entire Universe has been created on the substratum (Adhiṣṭhāna, अधिष्ठान) of Brahman. Hence Brahman is the most primeval principle (Ādi), which transcends the three times (past, present and future).
- Īśvara - Vedānta says that the creator of the Universe is the God, i.e. Īśvara (Brahman + Māyā). Hence, Ādipuruṣa in this verse can mean Īśvara as well.

The God (Ādipuruṣa, आदिपुरुष) can be worshipped in two different ways -

1. Nirguṇa (निर्गुण) - Meditate on the principle that I and the God are essentially one in nature, i.e. Brahman. This requires guidance from Sadguru and dispassion of worldly objects. Sadguru has realized Brahman as the real Self. He alone can put all doubts to rest and satisfy seekers completely.
2. Saguṇa (सगुण) - Worship the God in the form of Lord Rāma, Lord Kṛṣṇa, etc. with love, affection, service, friendship and quiet meditation.

The eighth blessing in this verse has three different meanings -

1. **First Meaning:**

In this prayer, Jñāneśwara Mahārāja is praying for Pure, Absolute Bliss, which exists eternally.

किंबहुना सर्व सुखी । पूर्ण होऊनि तिहीं लोकी ।

Kiṁbahunā sarva sukhī | Pūrṇa hoūni tinhīṁ lokī |

Earlier, in the sixth blessing (3rd verse), he has expressed his wish about worldly happiness for one and all -

जो जे वांछील तो तें लाहो । प्राणिजात ॥

Jo je vāñchīla to teṁ lāho | Prāṇijāta || 3 ||

- 'May everyone get what he or she wishes for.'

The worldly happiness (expressed in sixth blessing) depends on material objects, people, events and circumstances. It is not constant and eternal. However,

Pure Bliss of Self-realization (Brahman) (expressed in eighth blessing, 7th verse) does not ever change or depend on anything.

In this seventh verse, Sant Jñāneśwara asks the blessing (commitment) from all of us that we become Brahman or Pure Bliss in ourselves. The word '**Sarva Sukhī**' here does not mean that we should strive to acquire all material objects or sense pleasures. According to Vedānta, happiness from all worldly objects derives from the substratum of Brahman, which is Pure Bliss.

There is a specific reason why we feel happy when we acquire worldly objects. The mind first desires to enjoy an object. For example, we crave for a cup of tea in morning, especially in winter. When we drink piping hot, aromatic tea, it makes us very happy. So, we naturally think that 'tea provides happiness'. In reality, the desire to drink tea gets fulfilled and mind becomes quiet as a result. Vedānta says that the mind (Antaḥkaraṇa, अंतःकरण) gets dissolved when a desire is fulfilled. Hence, Pure Bliss is manifested. Pure Bliss (Ātmasukha, आत्मसुख) is eternally existent and available. However, it is hidden and covered due to incessant thoughts and activities in the mind. When mind becomes quiet after enjoying a sense object (such as tea), the Pure Bliss inside us gets manifested. We mistakenly assume that the experience of happiness is due to external object. Vedānta propounds that Pure Bliss can be experienced by everyone independently, without presence or absence of any worldly object.

Sant Jñāneśwara expresses a wish that we (readers) commit ourselves to the path of Self-realization and realize Pure Bliss in the process. This is the only way to attain permanent totality or completeness in life. Any discerning person can understand that completeness achieved using worldly objects or measures can quickly turn into incompleteness. Extrinsic objects such as branded clothes, perfumes, watches or shows cannot make a man feel complete intrinsically. Material completeness can be damaged easily with factors such as accidents, diseases, theft, natural calamities, feuds, death, wars, revolutions, hooliganism, corruption and many more. There are many examples of destruction of life, houses, money and business due to tornadoes, hurricanes, cyclones, floods or storms in different parts of the world. Experiences of misery and fearfulness are inescapable while we are dependent on worldly objects or people for happiness. Every human is constrained with three illusions that 'I am body', 'the world is real', and 'I am the doer and enjoyer'. To be 'complete' and 'happy' in true sense, we need to slowly liberate ourselves from the clutches of these illusions. Realization that 'I am the complete, omnipresent, omnipotent, Eternal Brahman' is the only way to feel complete in life. When a seeker worships Īśvara with utmost surrender and selflessness, his spiritual pursuit comes to an end, and he becomes one with Brahman. Sant Jñāneśwara recommends that even after enlightenment, one should continue to worship Īśvara with faith and devotion. Īśvara genuinely likes it when realized saints lovingly worship Him. Sant Jñāneśwara thus recommends that the seeker continues to worship Īśvara both before and after Self-realization.

2. Second Meaning:

This prayer also suggests that one should devotedly worship the God even after having all worldly comforts. One should not become conceited after amassing enormous wealth and power and forget the God. Famous Indian kings such as Rukmāṅgada, Ambarīṣa, Vibhīṣaṇa and Śivājī were devoted to the God. They lifted themselves to experience Pure Bliss despite all the lures of kingly comforts. On the contrary, kings like Rāvaṇa and Duryodhana met with destruction, since they were pompous and arrogant. Wealth, knowledge and power are the three sources of conceit and vanity. These traits override thoughtfulness, balance and wisdom. Even Lord Brahmadeva, who created the Universe was bestowed with knowledge and devotion (Jñāna with Bhakti), so that he would not get infected with pride and arrogance.

In the pursuit of life full of worldly enjoyments, one should lovingly remember God and persistently chant his Name (NāmaSmaraṇa, नामस्मरण). One should keep unwavering faith in saints, their texts and scriptures. One must help the powerless, weak, sick, underprivileged, physically challenged, oppressed and downtrodden people. Everybody is indebted to the society. All people in the society are unavoidably interdependent and interconnected. Hence, one must spend a part of his fortune for the betterment of the society. Jñāneśwara Mahārāja says that, 'All earnings should be taken as instruments of worship and spent accordingly on Swadharma (Duty-Based Religion).'

3. Third Meaning:

Sant Jñāneśwara also prays for a blessing in this verse by which, enlightened people who have realized the real Self and attained blissful existence, should guide others for the rest of their lives. Personally, they enjoy unprecedented bliss of love of Īśvara (with name and form). Socially they serve as compasses to the travelers on the path of Pure Bliss.

All the three implied meanings of this verse are important from personal, social and political perspective.

Why worship Īśvara?

A few theorists think that the Universe has been created from insentient (Jaḍa, जड) matter. However, creation of the world is an inconceivable process. The elements of the nature operate in a specific, conducted and directed manner. It is irreconcilable to think that such organized and harmonious Universe has been created from an insentient entity. Few other theorists advocate Śūnya (शून्य) or nothingness (Abhāva, अभाव) as the source of the Universe. But anything nonexistent cannot be the cause of something that evidently exists.

Thus, it is easily seen that the omnipotent, omniscient Īśvara is the cause or the creator of the Universe. That is why He should be worshipped. He is the most primeval (Ādi, आदि) and eternal principle, i.e. Brahman. If the world does not have a beginning (denoted by the word Ādi) and a creator (denoted by the word Puruṣa), then the visible world cannot be substantiated in any manner.

Īśvara has done a highly benevolent job of creating the five great elements (PañcaMahābhūta, पंचमहाभूत), mind, intellect and the ego. He has created the very first machine in the form of human body and most primeval regulation in the form of Vedas.

There are two branches of Science.

<u>Fundamental Science</u> – Earth, wind, rain, fire, sky (ether), mind, intellect and ego are the eight fundamental elements of this Universe. All modern, experimental sciences are based on the combination of these elements. No scientist has created these basic 8 elements of the nature. Inventions of various metals, minerals, steam, electricity, thermal and atomic energy have evolved from these 8 elements. Only because of the 'mind', humans have a desire to invent something new. The 'intellect' helps in comprehension of the 'Cause and Effect' law in the Universe. It is the 'intellect' that helps in final decision-making process. The 'ego' is the very driving force behind every human action. The mind, intellect and ego are all creations of the God. The very words, 'research', 'discovery' explain the fact that scientists

merely search for what already exists in the Universe. They can only rediscover the existing knowledge, which is hidden in form.

Derived Science – Human body is an example of built-up Science. It emerges from the mutation of male and female eggs, which are originally created from the five great elements (PañcaMahābhūta) and food. Man rides on this body by means of his ego (man starts thinking that I am body), and Īśvara regulates every Jīva (embodies soul) with the Law of Karma. Thus, the machine of human body becomes capable of working, enjoying, suffering, creating and destroying. Twenty-four principles of Sāṅkhya, sixteen of Naiyāyikas and seven of Vaiśeṣikas are all drawn from these basic eight elements.

The Vedas were created to describe this omnipresent Puruṣa (Īśvara). He (Īśvara) ensures that human beings enjoy or suffer strictly according to their own Karma. Scriptures were created to explain the Law of Karma. Languages and grammar were created because humans were given ability to communicate. Medicinal properties of various plants, herbs were discovered for curing diseases, which led to the evolution of Medical Science. Commerce evolved mainly due to the presence of gold and silver. Oil, cotton and cereals were created from the earth. The concepts of Geometry originated from the earth as well. Astronomy was created due to the presence of the sun, the moon and other planets such as Mercury,

Venus, etc. Geography was created due to presence of the earth, rivers, mountains and oceans. Thus, everything that is man-made is based on the elements created by Īśvara.

Every person, believer or atheist, is a part of the same Īśvara. People derive their knowledge and power from Him. A small village head has certain authority, which he exercises over his jurisdiction. But that power is ultimately drawn from the Central Government. In the same way, every power in the human realm, big or small, is ultimately drawn from the omnipotent, all-powerful Īśvara. Hence, everyone should worship Him for His final, greatest authority and power in the world.

NINTH PRAYER

The eighth verse has two blessings. The verse is -

आणि ग्रंथोपजीविये । विशेषीं लोकीं इयें ।
दृष्टादृष्ट विजयें । होआवे जी ॥ ८ ॥

Āṇi granṭhopajīviye | Viśeṣīṁ lokīṁ iyeṁ |
Dṛṣṭādṛṣṭa vijayeṁ | Hoāve jī || 8 ||

- 'Followers of scriptures and pious texts (should be victorious in this world and beyond).' (9th prayer)

This is the last part of prayers by Sant Jñāneśwara. This is an inspirational verse, where readers are given the responsibility to live life according to the guidance of scriptures, while Īśvara has the responsibility to give people suitable results according to their Karma (Actions). The word **Granṭhopajīviye** in this verse is quite peculiar. **Granṭha** (ग्रंथ) means scriptures. **Upajīvana** (उपजीवन) means livelihood or sustenance. **Granṭhopajīvan** (ग्रंथोपजीवन) means living life in accordance with the message and teachings of scriptures such as Jñāneśwarī, Bhagvad Gītā or Upaniṣads. It does not surely mean that one can earn his 'bread and butter' merely by studying these scriptures. It indicates that the path of life expounded by scriptures leads to both material welfare (Abhyudaya; अभ्युदय) and spiritual progress (Niḥśreyas; निःश्रेयस).

Only human beings have the freedom to choose between superficial life dominated by worldly desires and profound life expounded by scriptures. They must exercise that freedom and choose the best possible way of life that leads them to Eternal, Pure, Supreme Bliss. Lord Kṛṣṇa has given comprehensive guidance to Arjuna in Gītā. However, in the end he has clearly said –

यथेच्छसि तथा कुरु ।

Yathecchasi tatha kuru /

- 'Do what you wish to do.'

Scriptures on Advaita Vedānta such as Bhagvad-Gītā, Upaniṣads, Mahābhārata, Rāmāyaṇa, Bhāgwata and commentaries by Ādi Śaṅkarācārya, are considered as the ultimate authoritative texts. These books lead the human beings towards complete welfare, peace and Pure Bliss in life. People should read and study these texts under the guidance of enlightened Sadguru. Those who follow the teachings of these sacred books in their lives, be blessed with both material and spiritual happiness.

It has become a fashion these days to ridicule and denounce those who advocate scriptures. However, even such people have to follow some code of conduct, statutes, penal codes, political treatises and many legal white papers. All these other types of documents evolve and change continuously. Today's faith is tomorrow's folly. Scriptures and texts written by saints, however, stay eternally relevant, valuable and constant in nature.

Sant Jñāneśwara has earlier described good and bad actions, sins, sinners and Swadharma in Pasāyadāna. He has also described genuine good-will and friendship amongst human beings. Does friendship mean merry-making, eating and drinking together? Does it mean playing and relaxing in each other's company? Does it mean helping each other in business, elections and other activities? Or, is spiritual friendship different from the established norms? What is the definition of the God and devotion (Bhakti)? What is Pure Bliss and how to worship the God? What is the importance of Self-realized saints, sages and seeking their company? Such questions are accurately answered in the sacred books in a convincing manner.

Therefore, everyone should study these texts with utmost dedication, sincerity and constructive inquisitiveness. Without following teachings from these books, human beings cannot live a completely peaceful and blissful life. This is the main aim of asking the Ninth Blessing.

TENTH PRAYER

The final prayer is -

दृष्टादृष्ट विजयें । होआवे जी ॥ (10th prayer)

Dṛṣṭādṛṣṭa vijayeṁ | Hoāve jī ||

- '(Follower of scriptures and pious texts should) be victorious in this world and beyond.'

Scriptures, Guru, saints or Īśvara can provide guidance. However, a person must learn these texts and act in his own interests (Kriyamāṇa Karma Swātantrya, क्रियमाण कर्म स्वातंत्र्य). Everyone must endure both good and bad times as dictated by destiny (Prārabdha, प्रारब्ध). However, it is possible to learn how to handle good or bad situations effectively and thoughtfully with the help of the saintly texts and Vedānta scriptures. The practitioner of these texts stays in equipoised state through all good or bad circumstances. This is the real nature of Dṛṣṭa Vijaya (दृष्ट विजय), which means success in the material world.

The word Vijaya (विजय) in this verse literally stands for 'victory'. However, Sant Jñāneśwara does not just indicate 'being victorious in this competitive world, earning loads of material wealth and enjoying it to the fullest' in this verse. It is not necessary that every seeker would get success or victory in worldly life. However, every seeker can surely attain a state of equipoise and calmness in worldly activities. Real victory lies in eradicating the desire or tendency to amass worldly objects and wealth. Sant Jñāneśwara thus delicately unfolds this meaning of the word 'victory in worldly matters' (Dṛṣṭa Vijaya, दृष्ट विजय) for us here.

The word Adṛṣṭa (अदृष्ट) stands for Mokṣa or liberation or Self-realization. This is the final outcome of the study of Jñāneśwarī.

Seekers who have scrupulously followed the sacred texts, obeyed directives of the saints, acquired positive and divine traits, performed all their duties in a selfless manner, loved and prayed to the God, mastered their mind, practiced thoughtful detachment and achieved complete knowledge of the real Self, should be able to see the Ultimate God (Brahman). They should reach the stage of Self-realization and know that they themselves are the same as the God (Brahman) in essence.

Sant Jñāneśwara has used the word 'Victory' (Vijaya, विजय) with a very specific purpose. There is a saying-

श्रेयांसि बहुविघ्नानि ।

Śreyāṅsi bahuvighnāni |

- 'Everything that is beneficial and good is studded with hardships and obstacles.'

If we achieve something without resistance, obstacles or calamities, it really cannot be qualified as an achievement. Negative traits in mind such as lust, anger etc. are the inner barriers, while malicious people are the external barriers. These barriers destroy both spiritual and material welfare of human beings.

Sant Jñāneśwara asks for removal of all hurdles, hardships, obstructions and resistance on the path of those who follow the teachings of scriptures. Seekers on the path of Self-realization should not be deprived of anything that is considered glorious, delightful or enchanting. They should not be feeble, oppressed, miserable, agitated, restless or discontent in life. Ultimately everyone should evolve and reach the stage of Self-realization, which is the epitome of a meaningful, elevated and triumphant human-life.

BLESSING BY THE GURU

Traditional Meaning

When the disciple prays for such sublime blessings for the entire Universe, the Guru is bound to be pleased. Sant Nivṛttinātha was known to be graceful and his Guru Sant Gahininātha had ordered him to lead many people to their ultimate welfare, i.e. liberation (Mokṣa, मोक्ष) in Kaliyuga. Sant Jñāneśwara was the only disciple of Sant Nivṛttinātha. Sant Jñāneśwara was devoted, dutiful, and he selflessly pined for the upliftment of the entire Universe. Hence, Sant Nivṛttinātha readily blessed his favorite disciple in this last verse -

येथ म्हणे श्रीविश्वेशरावो । हा होईल दानपसावो ।
येणें वरें ज्ञानदेवो । सुखिया जाला ॥ ९ ॥

Yetha mhaṇe śrī Viśveśarāvo | Hā hoīla dāna pasāvo |
Yeṇeṁ vareṁ Jṅyānadevo | Sukhiyā jālā || 9 ||

Here Sant Nivṛttinātha, who was the Lord in the Universal form, said to Sant Jñāneśwara that his prayers will indeed be heard and fulfilled. With this divine, blissful grace from Sadguru, Sant Jñāneśwara was truly gratified and happy. His happiness genuinely involved seeing the welfare of the entire Universe. He had a firm belief that his prayers in Pasāyadāna were meant for everyone in the world.

The blessings granted by Sant Nivṛttināthа did not include worldly, mundane matters such as real-estate, gold, money, clothing etc. In fact, these endowments were meant to change the very mindset of all people in the world to make them more friendly, helpful and benevolent. Sant Jñāneśwara, thus became completely content with these divine blessings by his Śadguru.

New Light

It is imperative that Pasāyadāna not be just looked as the 'give and take' phenomenon between a Guru and his disciple. All readers and seekers must assume the responsibility of studying texts such as Pasāyadāna, Bhagvad-Gītā, Jñāneśwarī and change their own behavior intrinsically. It is incorrect to passively rely on the blessing of Sant Nivṛttinātha and expect miraculous change in the society or mankind. Each one of us has the accountability to first eliminate his own evil tendencies, rectify sinful behavior, meticulously execute all duties, and then help other people in society on the path of Pure Bliss outlined by Pasāyadāna. Only then, we can rightfully say that Divine Blessings asked by Sant Jñāneśwara have been culminated in real sense.

CONCLUSION

This commentary attempts to look at Pasāyadāna from a new perspective. It is written with a strong emphasis on what a seeker should be doing rather than just passively asking blessings from Īśvara or Guru. Idealism has been coupled with practical aspects. There is a sincere effort to awaken all seekers towards their own responsibilities for both material and spiritual growth.

Indiscreet behavior in any area of life is clearly not desirable. It eventually leads to debacle and complete ruin. Ancient Indian philosopher Manu says -

कामात्मना न प्रशस्ता ।

Kāmātmanā na praśastā |

- 'Following all the desires in the mind is not recommended.'

Animals naturally follow their innate instincts. But, it is unbecoming of humans when they do the same. However, it is a fact that, not all humans will be dispassionate for worldly life and pleasures like Ādi Śaṅkarācārya, or celibate like Lord Hanumana, or saints like Śri Tukārāma. But every human being can gradually evolve towards sainthood by following his duties, scriptures, Vedānta treatises and the texts written by enlightened saints.

Everyone should be aware of the vast difference between a beast and a human, so that he can lead himself to enlightenment. Nature has given complete freedom to human beings to be judicious and choose the correct path of action. One who follows his beastly instincts destroys himself just like a monkey, who has a burning torch in his hands. One who uses prudent thinking can lead himself to his ultimate welfare, i.e. Self-realization. It is up to the humans to make discreet use of their freedom and follow the right path in life.

With this in mind, Sant Jñāneśwara requests his Sadguru to grace humans with these blessings-

1. May the evil, vicious people shed their wickedness.
2. May the darkness of sins and immoral behavior disappear.
3. May everybody be gradually inclined to pious and noble deeds.
4. May the sun of Swadharma (Duty-Based Religion) rise upon the Universe.
5. May all living beings be bonded by the ties of friendly companionship.
6. May the entire humanity meet gracious, righteous and noble saints.

7. May everyone be devoted to the all-pervasive Lord in the Universal Form.
8. May everyone live by the divine scriptures.
9. May the followers of divine, pious texts be victorious in this world and beyond.
10. May all worldly and spiritual aspirations of all beings be fulfilled.

In brief, a human being should stay away from beastly behavior. He should progressively follow self-duties, Religion (duties), teachings of the saints and devote himself to the quest of the real God. He should gradually evolve from being a human to saint, and ultimately realize Oneness with the God. This is the real upliftment and epitome of human life. Sant Jñāneśwara believes that one needs appropriate resources as well as eligibility for progress in both worldly and spiritual realms. An ineligible, inept or unskillful person cannot find success or prosperity even in his mundane life.

Prosperous worldly life does not just mean wealth, power, fame, mansion, luxuries, good health, high qualification, illustrious family and reputation in the society. If a person is corrupt or unrighteous, then his life is bound to be distressful despite being full of luxuries and glories. A persistently malicious person cannot enjoy worldly prosperity and spiritual upliftment in his current as well as next births. He brings misfortune upon himself, his family, and acquaintances. If a leader himself is vicious in nature, he leads the entire nation to destruction. On the contrary, it can be said that even poverty shines like an ornament in the presence of righteousness.

Personal and social life is mainly meant for contentment and happiness. Prosperity on national level indicates industrial, commercial and social growth. Growth is dependent on persistent and steadfast efforts. However, hard-work cannot alone bring the welfare of an individual or nation. Judicious execution of self-duties and the grace of the God (Īśvara) play an equally important role in this matter. Arjuna was a prudent follower of his own duties, and he had complete support of Lord Kṛṣṇa. Therefore, he could defeat vicious Duryodhana. When leaders are dutiful, religious and prudent followers of the teachings of saints and Vedānta, then they lead their own units, families and entire nations to victories in on all fronts.

In brief, we need Swadharma (Duty-Based Religion), guidance of saints and grace of Īśvara for success and prosperity even in everyday life. For seekers on spiritual path, it is even more important to follow the guidelines of righteousness, self-duties and Religion.

One may be skeptical that modern day India is secular, passive and indifferent towards traditional concepts of Religion. However, Lord Kṛṣṇa has himself said in Bhagvad-Gītā -

धर्मसंस्थापनार्थाय सम्भवामि युगे युगे ।

Dharma-saṁsthāpanārthāya-sambhavāmi yuge yuge |

- 'I myself appear to re-establish the principles of Religion in every millennium.'

One may question the very definition of the word 'Religion' here. What is so special about Religion that the God and saints consistently pine and toil to create the foundation of Religion in the society? Religion has been traditionally useful in the old-era to curb immoral behavior and keep people away from sinful, vicious actions. However, what is the use and value of such Religion for today's intellectual generation?

These questions can be answered if we evaluate the original definition of the word 'Religion' here.

धारणात् धर्ममित्याहुः ।

Dhāraṇāt Dharmamityāhuḥ |

- 'A system that establishes peaceful, stable, righteous thinking on an individual, social and governmental level is called as Religion.'

Even in modern age of Science, nobody can deny the significance of righteous thinking in the society. But such thinking cannot be enforced by law and order. It needs to be imbibed in the psyche of the entire society intrinsically.

It is equally important that the innate desires, ambitions and aspirations of people be fulfilled. Most ordinary people cannot become detached or dispassionate by themselves. A select few people develop the ability to detach in the company of saints. Ordinary people need material objects for their enjoyment. They also feel that they should be able to enjoy these objects without any hassles, fear or worries. They have a genuine wish to not create obstacles in the path of others in the society while enjoying their own lives. For this, Ādi Śaṅkarācārya has written one more definition of 'Religion'-

प्राणिनां साक्षादभ्युदयनिःश्रेयसहेतुः स धर्मः ।

Praṇinām Sākṣādabhyudayaniḥśreyasahetuḥ sa dharmaḥ /

- 'The system that enables ordinary people find worldly pleasures and luxuries, and seekers find the eternal Pure Bliss of liberation (Mokṣa, मोक्ष) is called as Religion.'

This definition aptly portrays both the beauty and necessity of Religion.

In brief, the society will not find peaceful and stable social and political ambience unless it is rooted in the concept of Religion as portrayed above. In the absence of Religion, people will not be able to enjoy the luxuries in a smooth, unruffled manner. Society will be infected with self-indulgence and frivolity.

There are three main reasons for the non-sustenance of righteousness in the society. They are -

1. Unrestrained desires or lust (Kāma, काम)
2. Anger (Krodha, क्रोध)
3. Greed (Lobha, लोभ)

These three negative traits cannot be controlled just by law and order. Only Religion, as portrayed by the definitions above, is capable of fighting with these three traits from the society. Religion can regulate, constrain, dispose of, or eradicate these negative traits from human mind.

1. Regulation of Negative traits

Desires, anger and greed are deceptive traits that slowly destroy the beauty, piousness, truth and decorum of human life. They transform a person from being virtuous to vicious.

- The subject of lust is woman (or man).
- The subject of anger is opponent (unfavorable person).
- The subject of greed is money.

When Religion does not regulate these three traits and their subjects, the entire code of righteous conduct collapses. For example -

- Lust grows rampantly if it is not regulated by Religion. People indulge openly in frivolous conduct, infidelity or molestation.
- If Religion does not regulate anger, then a raging, furious person may kill his own family members,

friends or other acquaintances. When anger proliferates in the society, it creates enmity between two parties, which leads to violence, assault and rampage amongst people. With the presence of mass media, situation quickly worsens due to antipathy, bitterness, processions, protests, antagonistic news and other hostile activities. If political leaders succumb to raging anger, then they try to destroy the opposition parties with undue laws and regulations. When national leaders fall prey to uncontrollable fury or wrath, it leads to giant world-wars between nations. Many innocent people get killed in these circumstances. This is the harsh reality of life.

- If Religion does not regulate greed, then an excessively greedy person runs after wealth. He tries to amass loads of money by mending rules, violating laws, deceiving people, mal-practicing in business, bribing, stealing, robbing, smuggling or using other illicit practices. The commercial system collapses. Honest law-abiding citizens suffer for no reason in such situations.

Thus, righteousness on all levels takes a backseat due to these three negative traits. Religion can curb and eradicate these traits in following ways -

- When lust is regulated by Religion, people will stay automatically loyal to their spouses and not indulge in infidelity. The progeny born out of such healthy marriages and families will be automatically strong, intelligent, wise, devoted and conscientious.

- When anger is regulated by Religion, it leads to lawful Government in the nation. When angry parents scold their child, it is meant only to keep him away from bad conduct and channelize him on the path of success and virtuosity. Teachers getting angry with their students is an example of good administration. When political leaders punish thieves, robbers, pirates, looters or criminals, it is a sign of good administration as well. When wise, erudite scholars sternly explain the policies and code of conduct to the national leaders, that too is a part of valuable administration. All these examples of manifestations of (controlled) anger are appropriate and justifiable. They are in fact necessary for untroubled social life.
- When greed is regulated by Religion, then even a greedy person tries to discriminate between virtuous – sinful behavior, legal–illegal conduct, and ethical–non-ethical practices while earning money. He also donates his excess money to charity, and social or noble causes, which maintains the financial balance in the society.

Selfless work, studies of scriptures, company of wise sages and consistent spiritual practices can together help to control the negative traits of lust, anger and greed.

2. Constraining Negative traits

In Aṣṭāṅga Yoga, the mind can be constrained with the help of 8 steps of Yoga such as Yama, Niyama, Prāṇāyāma, etc. When the mind is under complete control, the negative traits of lust, anger and greed are automatically eradicated. However, Aṣṭāṅga Yoga may be too difficult to practice for many ordinary people. They can follow the Religion of Devotion (Bhāgvata Dharma, भागवत धर्म).

3. Disposing of Negative Traits

The loving desire of Gopis, anger of Śiśupāla and ardent love of Prahlāda, Nārada were channelized towards various incarnations of the God. Their negative traits were disposed of. They could reach the stage of Self-realization.

4. Eradication of Negative Traits

Ignorance of the real Self is the root of traits like lust, anger and greed. After Self-realization, ignorance is completely eradicated, and negative traits are automatically wiped out. A Self-realized person sees only Brahman in himself and all other beings. The desire to enjoy luxuries or sense pleasures is completely wiped out at this stage. He is equipoised when looking at both his old enemy and friend. They are both Brahman to him, since anger is completely eradicated. Gold and dust mean the same to him. Greed is destroyed from his mind.

Thus, Religion constrains lust, greed and anger in four different ways. Self-realization is the best way amongst the four ways mentioned above.

Indian saints have constantly and attentively toiled to establish and protect the ground of this expansive and all-inclusive idea of Religion. They led exemplary lives that are highly decorous and respectable. Ādi Śaṅkarācārya was an erudite sage, renunciate scholar and foremost proponent of Advaita Vedānta, who traveled the entire country barefoot with mere one piece of cloth. He was especially known for his unrivaled talent in theological debate. He faced other established debaters and scholars based on logic and authoritative verses in Upaniṣads to establish the supreme authority of Advaita Vedānta at the time. Sant Jñāneśwara, Sant Eknātha, Lord Rāma, Sītā, Lakṣman-Bharata are all known for their remarkable ethics, ideals and supreme wisdom.

It is indeed beneficial to live human life with unwavering allegiance to the teachings of Vedas and divine power of the God. However, it is evidently not possible in today's age of Science. The modern generation does not have the required faith in spiritual teachings. However, Vedas are the national treasure of India and they are highly credible texts. Judicious execution of self-duties is a well-known tradition of Indian people. Saints are the valuable gems of the Indian land. At least Indian people can follow teachings of saints and Vedas. The glory and impact of following one's duties (Swadharma) in India will gradually traverse and enlighten the entire world.

A nation should progress in the field of science, technology and finances. However, it is also necessary that national, social and political leaders operate in a righteous and moral manner. Pasāyadāna has outlined multiple strategies to bring about this intrinsic change in the collective mindset of people.

The evolution of society and nation portrayed n Pasāyadāna is vast, expansive and profound in nature. Moreover, it is presented in the light of the divine power of God (Īśvaravāda, ईश्वरवाद). Sant Jñāneśwara has first made everyone notice the presence of subtle, transcendental, divine power of the God (Īśvara), and then think about technological and commercial progress of the nation. He has urged mankind to attentively think about the creator of luxuries rather than just enjoying those luxuries. He has asked people to take refuge in the shelter of selfless, benevolent saints rather than just staying cocooned in the selfish circle of friends and relatives. People who follow these teachings will be unaffected from malicious thinking and unrighteous actions in their lives. They will be more conscious and discriminative about justice-injustice, virtuous-sinful actions etc. They will naturally stay away from bribery, violence, frivolousness, viciousness, robbery, theft, addictions and contemptible behavior. The society will intellectually elevate itself. People who believe in the teachings of saints and scriptures, will see that their lives, actions and results (of actions) are pious, prosperous, stable, perpetual and joyous in nature.

Sant Jñāneśwara has asked the divine, sublime blessing for evolution of Swadharma (Duty-Based Religion) in his Pasāyadāna. His Guru Sant Nivṛttinātha, who is aware of the preciousness of Swadharma, has graciously conceded and granted the same blessing. As readers, it is our prime responsibility to consciously lead our lives in the glorious pathway outlined by Pasāyadāna.

~ About Editor ~

Dr. Shrikrishna Deshmukh, fondly called as Dr. Kaka, is a disciple of the author Shri Shankar Maharaj Khandarkar. A retired Medical Practitioner revered by many people for his selfless, exemplary medical service, Dr. Kaka hails from a town named Murgud in Kolhapur district in Maharashtra. He is a renowned spiritual teacher and exponent of Advaita Vedānta.

He has authored more than 50 books in Marathi on topics including Upaniṣads, Bhagavad-Gītā and Brahmasūtras. He is known for his remarkable dexterity in logically analyzing intricate concepts of Vedānta. An excellent orator, he emphasizes the path of 'Applied Vedanta' in day-to-day life and his lectures resonate extremely well with audiences of all ages.

Today, many Truth-seekers are drawn towards him due to his wisdom, compassion and practical approach towards spirituality. His cheerful, calm, reticent and courteous nature is highly revered and genuinely admired by one and all.

- More Info, Books and Lectures:
  http://shankarmaharajkhandarkar.org/
  http://vedantbhaskar.org
  http://www.shrikrupaprakashan.com/
- Select Hindi and English Translations:
  http://vedantbhaskar.blogspot.in